THE
ABUNDANCE
PARADIGM

T0150972

Also by Dr. Joe Vitale

Faith

Expect Miracles

Zero Limits

The Miracle

The Art and Science of Results

The Fifth Phrase

Karmic Marketing

THE
ABUNDANCE
PARADIGM

MOVING FROM
THE LAW OF ATTRACTION TO
THE LAW OF CREATION

DR. JOE VITALE

MEDIA

Published 2022 by Gildan Media LLC
aka G&D Media
www.GandDmedia.com

Front cover design by David Rheinhardt of Pyrographx

Interior design by Meghan Day Healey of Story Horse, LLC

Library of Congress Cataloging-in-Publication Data is available upon request

ISBN: 978-1-7225-0554-7

10   9   8   7   6   5   4   3   2   1

To Lisa Winston

Contents

1

Four Stages of Awakening

What do you really want? You want happiness. You want peace. You're chasing what you think is going to deliver it.

Most people think if they have more time, more money, more cars, more houses, or a better job, they'll be happy; they'll be at peace.

That's the grand illusion. What you really want is right here in this moment. You may not understand it right now, but as you go through this book and the clearing processes in it, you'll reach an insight that'll be very real. It'll bring about a mind shift for you, and it will show you that peace, miracles, happiness, and everything else you want are all right here in this moment.

When you have the abundance paradigm as a permanent mental shift in your awareness, you no longer have to think about it. In fact, time becomes a watery, limitless dimension, and money comes to you easily and effortlessly, because you see it everywhere, and you see opportunities everywhere. Peace is no longer something that comes to you, because you live it: you realize it's in this particular moment.

As we go through the abundance paradigm, all of this will become crystal clear, because the paradigm you are in right now will shift into the abundance paradigm. I'm excited for you. As I often tell people, "Expect miracles, because here they come."

The abundance paradigm is going teach you how to move from the law of attraction to the law of creation. In this book, I'm going to take you through a personal transformation—a mind shift.

First, however, let me tell you a little bit about myself. I was in Rhonda Byrne's celebrated 2006 movie *The Secret* and after that went on to many other movies, including *The Compass*, *Try It on Everything*, *The Tapping Solution*, *The Meta Secret*, *The Leap*, and many other ones. I've been on various television shows including Larry King and Donny Deutsch, and I've been on ABC, CBS, CNN, and Fox News. I've written numerous books, including about fifty-three titles in marketing, advertising, publicity, spirituality, inspiration, and self-help.

I've also recorded numerous audio programs, including *The Power of Outrageous Marketing*, the best-selling *Missing Secret*, *The Secret to Attracting Money*, and *The Awakening*. I'm a certified hypnotherapist, a certified qi gong healer, and a certified Reiki master. I'm an ordained minister. I have two PhDs, one in marketing and one in metaphysical science. I also have my own radio show on CBS Radio called *The Joe Vitale Radio Show*. I'm also an explorer of the mystique traditions from ancient cultures. I've been all over the world from Russia to Peru to Poland and points between, always looking for ways to help us awaken and experience the paradigm shift that we need.

That brings me to this material. It is leading-edge, breakthrough material. It is information and inspiration I have not shared before. I haven't shared it before, because I needed to prepare people for it.

Hopefully, you've read other books or listened to other programs by me. Whether you have or have not, I'll bring you up to speed, and then I'll take you to a place that's called the abundance paradigm.

First of all, what is a paradigm? A paradigm is a mindset. It's not just a belief; it's a collection of beliefs. It's your way of looking at the world. Your paradigm is so much a part of your personality right now that you don't even know what it is. You just take it for your reality. Life is the way it is for you because of the paradigm—the glasses you're wearing—because of the mindset, the framing you have due to the beliefs you've collected ever since you were a child.

Thomas Kuhn, the physicist and historian of science, is credited with coining the term *paradigm shift* in his famous book *The Structure of Scientific Revolutions*, published in 1962. Here we're talking about a paradigm shift in your life. We're not talking about science so much as about personal transformation.

Although there is science behind personal transformation, I'm here to help you get closer to awakening. I'm here to help you go from the law of attraction to the law of creation. In order to do that, I'll have to talk a little bit about both of these laws. My explanations are designed to help you move into a different understanding about abundance, your life, and what's possible for you. This different understanding is, of course, the paradigm shift I want you to have. That's the promise and essence of this book.

Let's jump into this material right now. Where are you going to be at the end of it, after you've completed the abundance paradigm? To help you understand that, I have to talk about the four stages of awakening.

If you're familiar with some of my previous works, you'll remember that I've talked about three stages of awakening. I only talked about three because in all honesty, that's all I knew at the time. Since writing those books and continuing to work on myself, my spiritual awakening has deepened. I've had satori experiences, which means I've had glimpses into this abundance paradigm, and I see that it's a process I can live. Because of that, I discovered the fourth stage of awakening.

Let me tell you what the four stages of awakening are. The first is *victimhood*. It's not really so much a stage of awakening; it's the stage into which most of us are born. When you're a victim, everybody is to blame for your life. Most people out there are living what Henry David Thoreau called "lives of quiet desperation," because they still feel like victims.

You might still have moments of feeling like a victim. However, at some point, you come across *The Secret*, my books, or somebody else's. You suddenly realize you don't need to be a victim anymore. Then you move into the second stage of awakening, which is *empowerment*. Now you take control of your life, and you start to manifest more of what you want. You start to feel some of your power; you start to feel some of what's possible for you. Empowerment is when you learn about the power of visualization, for example, or the power of intention. It certainly feels better than the first stage. Being a victim doesn't feel good at all, but feeling empowered feels wonderful.

If you've reached this second stage of awakening, you have a wonderful life—until something happens that you can't control. At that point, there's another kind of awakening, which I call *surrender*. At this third stage, you realize you do have power, but you don't have complete power. You are not in control of the planet. You are not God. You are not the Divine. You realize that you have to surrender to something more powerful than you. At this point, you surrender to a higher power, and you end up with more power than you ever thought you had.

However, there's a fourth stage: *awakening* itself. That's when you become the Divine. Although at first glance this may be difficult to understand, in this fourth stage, your ego dissolves and the Divine, or God, lives and breathes through you. You look around and realize that the world itself is abundant; you are part of this abundance; there is no scarcity, lack, or limitation. You can have, do, or be anything you want, because you *are* the very thing that you want to attract.

This principle goes beyond the law of attraction and moves into the law of creation. In this fourth state of awakening, you are now living the abundance paradigm. It's your new mindset, your new way of being. Your collection of beliefs have is now very much rooted in the Divine.

In the earlier stages, your beliefs and the way you were living your life were coming from your ego. There's nothing wrong with that in or of itself, except that there's more: you can awaken to a higher potential and a higher power.

You can awaken into living the abundance paradigm, and that's where I want to take you. I'm going to take you by the hand and lead you there. Right now, I'm trying to paint this picture so that you can visualize it. You can start to play with understanding what would it be like to live as Divinity breathing and acting through your body and mind. What would that be like? Take a moment to consider it, even if you don't understand it. Just tickle your unconscious mind with it. I'd like you to take a few moments and think about that right now.

Let's talk a little bit about the law of attraction and the law of creation, because the theme of this whole book is about moving from the law of attraction to the law of creation.

First of all, the law of attraction. Maybe you've heard about it, because it's been all over the world since the movie *The Secret*, which introduces this idea, has become so popular.

The law of attraction is the law saying that everything you have coming into your life is there because of your thoughts and feelings and beliefs. That's it, period. If you look around and if you like something or don't like something in your life, you have to look within and say, "The law of attraction brought it to me." If the law of attraction is a law—and it is—then what you have in your life is what you have attracted on some level within you. That's the essence of the law of attraction.

The problem with the law of attraction is that most people don't understand its depth. In fact, they become very critical of *The Secret* or any of the teachers of this law, because they say, "I saw the movie. I read the book. I practiced the law of attraction, and I didn't get what I want. It doesn't work."

The law of attraction does work, but you have to understand its deeper aspects. You don't necessarily get what you consciously want; you get what you unconsciously expect or believe. For example, you may say, "I intend to attract money. I intend to attract a relationship. I intend to attract more sales offers"—fill in the blank. Consciously, you can sit there, you can intend that, you can affirm it, you can visualize it, you can write it out a thousand times on a piece of paper. But you still won't get what you want if unconsciously you don't believe that it's possible, that you deserve it, that you're lovable or likable, that money is good, or that a relationship will ever happen to you. If you have unconscious intentions that run counter to what you say you want to attract, you will attract the counterintentions. When you get clear of the counterintentions, you can have, do, or be anything you can imagine. It's all about clearing.

In this book, I'm going to give you new, advanced clearing processes—ones that nobody has ever offered before. I have devised them based on my own experience,

I use them for myself personally, and I've talked about them to people in my Miracles Coaching Program, but up to this point I have never put them in writing. They are designed to do one thing: zap out of you any and all negativity and counterintentions to having or being whatever you've selected for yourself.

Many people have been infatuated with the law of attraction. Although it is something you need to know, understand, and use in your life, it's not the only law; there are others. What most people don't do with the law of attraction is take action, even though *action* is actually right in the word *attraction*. You have to take action for the law of attraction to work.

This leads us to the law of creation. The law of creation is all about taking action. Manifesting anything is a cocreation. It's you and the universe. It's you and the Divine. It's you and God. You participate in the creation of what you want.

When people look at my life and career, they seem astonished that I've been in so many movies, recorded so many audios, and written so many books. As of the present writing, I have written fifty-three books. Even I am in awe of this figure. How in the world did I write fifty-three books? I didn't start out with the intent of doing that; I started out with the intent of getting published. As I wrote the first book and learned about writing, publishing, and marketing, I started to write the second. As I started to write the second, I thought about a third. I just kept taking action.

As long as you take action, you will create. As long as you create, you will get results. As long as you're paying attention to those results, taking in feedback, and learning from it, you'll keep creating a wonderful, magical, even miraculous life.

The law of creation deals with bringing something into being. For example, when you have an idea for a product or service, it's only in the imaginary realm. It exists as a possibility. You can attract the idea into your life, and you may even attract the people to help you bring it about, but unless you act, either by yourself or with others, that idea will not become manifest. If it does, it'll be done by somebody else who did take action on it.

There are so many examples of this truth. People have created successful businesses during the Great Depression and during all the recessions we've gone through. You can probably even think of examples of your own where somebody got a wild idea and then went ahead and acted on it despite all the odds. Because they were engaging the law of creation, the universe, the Divine, or God, got on their side to help bring it into being.

The law of attraction in and of itself is not enough. This is why some people who are critical of the law of attraction don't understand its depth. They first need to understand that they're getting what they're thinking unconsciously.

Using the processes in this book, I'm going to show how to clear up these unconscious limiting beliefs.

The other law that helps you create this abundance paradigm is the law of creation. That means you must take some sort of action in order to bring into being this concept, this energy, this feeling, which has come to you as a gift.

I used to watch *The Donny Deutsch Show* on CNBC, and I was fortunate enough to be on it one time. I used to tell people to watch it because Donny was teaching entrepreneurs how to make a difference in their lives. He would bring people on the show who had no idea how to go into business. They had no experience, education, money, or resources, but they had an idea. They attracted it into their lives because they wanted it. That was the law of attraction, but then they had to do something, which is the law of creation.

One of my favorite stories had to do with a young woman from Florida who had an idea for a particular purse and went around trying to find somebody to make the prototype. She had the prototype made, and then she needed to find a manufacturer to make a number of them. She went online, did her Google research, and found out that the companies that could manufacture these purses for the least amount of money were in China.

Stop and think: what would you do at this point? She's a single woman. She doesn't speak Chinese. She doesn't have that much money. She put her investment into making the one prototype, and the company she needs to talk to is in China. What would you do?

This woman got on a plane, flew to China, went to a hotel, checked in, went to the front desk, and said, "I'm looking for these companies. Can you take me to them?" She then went to the companies and made cold calls on them. They didn't know she was coming. She did not speak Chinese. Although there were many learning curves and challenges, this woman got the deal she was looking for, and her purses were manufactured and distributed.

This woman faced her fears. She got clean and clear of anything in the way of her taking action. She used the law of attraction to bring the idea into her awareness and find the manufacturer she needed. But she also used the law of creation to take action, including flying overseas to a completely different world, and she accomplished her goals. She's now living the abundance paradigm because of that entrepreneurial shift.

This is a minor example of what's possible for you. You don't have to get on a plane and fly to China. You don't have to do anything death-defying. But you do have to stay the course. The combination of the law of attraction and the law of creation will help you shift into the abundance paradigm.

I have strategically designed this book to help you move through the process of awakening. You'll go through all four stages to end up at the fourth stage, which almost nobody is living in, but is possible for you—the stage where you're living the abundance paradigm. You're living with clarity, with the law of attraction, with power, with the law of creation. Everything happens easily and effortlessly.

I've been saying for many years that I've discovered the escalator through life. This escalator is under a big sign that says "The Abundance Paradigm."

Thirty-five years ago, I did not know about the abundance paradigm or the escalator through life. I was homeless on the streets of Dallas. It was very unpleasant. There were traumatic experiences that took me forever to erase and clear from my mind, but I've done it.

I was in poverty for well over ten years later, when I lived in Houston. I struggled. I took jobs that I hated. While I was working those jobs, I was listening to inspirational audios. Because I listened to those programs and worked on myself, I am here today, creating this book for you.

The message I hope you hear is one of inspiration. The more you work on yourself, the more you will transform yourself from where you are to where you want to be.

The good news is, this can happen in a heartbeat, because right now you're looking at life through a scarcity paradigm. When you start to look at your life through the abundance paradigm, you will see the escalator, and you will be on it through life. That's my personal promise to you.

To help you understand what paradigm you're in right now, ask yourself these questions: Do you ever have thoughts that you don't have enough money? Do you ever have thoughts that you don't have enough time? Do you ever have thoughts that you can't get what you want? Do you ever have thoughts that because of your parents, your family, your friends, the government, religion, or anybody else, your life can't be different? Have you ever had thoughts that say, there isn't enough to go around, let alone for you to have what you want? Have you ever had thoughts that you personally can't have what you want for any reason? Or that you're broken in some way?

All these thoughts are a form of self-talk that comes from a scarcity mindset. In other words, you were programmed to believe these things; most of us were. In that very first stage of awakening, called victimhood, we are brought into the world with some programming already in us from DNA and epigenetics. We quickly downloaded further information from our parents, our neighbors, our school system, the government, religion, media, and many other sources. All of these things are programming us.

Until you awaken to the second stage, which is empowerment, you feel there just isn't enough; it's you against the world. When I was homeless in Dallas, I felt it was me against the universe. There was nobody on my side. There was no money, no car, no house, no income, no job. There seemed to be no hope. That's a scarcity mindset.

Today I have a luxury lifestyle: I have a car collection and a guitar collection; I travel wherever I want. I have everything I want at my luxurious place in Texas; I get into the hot tub almost every night and give thanks to the stars for the life I have. That's the abundance paradigm.

If you're still in the scarcity mindset and you feel that there's not enough money or time or that this isn't going to work for you, just realize those are thoughts. Those are not facts. A fact is something that is measurable, that is reproduceable, that science can duplicate and study. Facts are things we can all agree on. Beliefs are very subjective: they are just thoughts that you've chosen to keep.

Not enough money? Obviously, there's more than enough money. Trillions of dollars are circulating in the world at any time. Not enough time? There's always time to do what you want to do. If you've moved into the abundance paradigm, you realize that time is an illusion. You can't get what you want? Maybe you haven't gotten what you've wanted *so far.* But as you move into the abundance paradigm and you learn more about the laws of attraction and creation, you will get all that you want and more. That's the Spirit. That's the living at the level of magic and miracles.

If you're at the scarcity right now, wonderful—wake up from it. Realize it's temporary. That's what you've had to wear in your life in the past. We're going to give you a new suit. We're going to give you a new paradigm.

Since we've been talking about a scarcity mindset, let me make something very clear to you. Let me help you understand how your mind is working right now. For example, pause and predict your next thought. Can you do it? No, you can't. You can tell me what your thought is only after it occurs to you. Why can't you predict it? Because it's not coming from your conscious mind; it's coming from your unconscious mind. Your thoughts are coming from the database where your paradigm is framed. If you're sitting there wondering, "I don't know if the program in this book is going to work for me," those thoughts are coming out of your unconscious mind. When you look at them after they've bubbled up, you notice that they're coming from a scarcity mindset.

Here's more good news: you have choice. I want to teach you the what-if-up process. This is a way to shift from the scarcity mindset to the abundance paradigm right now. You can do it in the next couple of minutes. You can do it as you're reading this book. You can do it out loud, on paper, or in your mind.

My friend Mendhi Audlin taught me the what-if-up process; she wrote a book called *What If It All Goes Right?* She learned this technique from inspirational speakers

Jerry and Esther Hicks. It enables you to choose to think positively.

What-if-down questions are questions like, "What if this program doesn't work for me?" You can tell it's a down question by noticing how you feel. If you start to feel that you don't have as much energy, you don't feel as happy, energetic, or enthusiastic, that's a what-if-down thought.

However, you can change these thoughts; you can go in the other direction. You can what-if-up everything. What if this book is giving you the greatest material you've ever gotten in your life? What if this is the greatest investment you've ever made? What if the processes in this book are so powerful, so unique, so leading-edge that they change you instantly? What if they have the answers to everything you've been seeking for your entire life?

Notice how you feel when you ask what-if-up questions. This is a way for you to move from the scarcity mindset into the abundance paradigm. Again, if you have negative thoughts, you can just say thanks and let them go by. As you move into the abundance paradigm, you're going to learn that negative thoughts are going to come and go, but you don't have to pay attention to them.

In one of the processes I'll be leading you through (which is a personal invention of mine), you're actually going to go to the place that's beyond thoughts. In this place, you can erase all of the data, the limiting beliefs, the scarcity paradigm that's been haunting you since you were born.

But for now, start with what-if-up thinking. It's sometimes called *up-spiral thinking*. Instead of thinking down, thinking negative, you turn it around, and you think positive. You will ask yourself, what would be better? What would be wonderful? What would be abundant? What would be great? What would be magical? What would be miraculous? Get into that mindset. The more you're in it, the closer you'll get to the abundance paradigm.

I'm enough of an entrepreneur to know that you want to take this material to the bank, to make it real in your own life. Since the law of creation is all about taking action, let's take some action right now. I'd like you to become aware of the next idea that comes to you—for a product, for a service, for a business, to make a phone call, to make a cold call, whatever it happens to be. You get ideas all the time, but most of us don't act on them. When an idea comes to you, what do you do with it? Most people talk themselves out of it. They say they don't have the time. They don't have the money. They're not the right person. They don't have the education. They don't have the experience. Does that sound like an abundance paradigm? No. That sounds like a scarcity paradigm.

From the standpoint of the law of creation, if you take action on those ideas as they come to you, you move into an abundance paradigm.

People ask me how I've been able to create so many books and audios. It's because I act on ideas as they come to me. Here's why. In the first place, when an idea comes to you, there's a great deal of passion and excitement. Aren't you thrilled with the idea? Don't you have a wonderful feeling that says, this could be big, this could be a moneymaker, this could be fun to do, this could bring joy the world? The energy that comes with the idea is available for you to use to manifest that idea, but only if you act right then and there.

In other words, when the idea comes to you, it's accompanied by a rush of energy. It's like running a marathon: that rush of energy gets behind you, gets in you, and helps you make the distance. When an idea comes to me to write or record something, I use the energy that came with the idea to propel me into getting it done. This is one of the magical things that happen when you use the law of creation and the law of attraction on your behalf.

In the second place, the universe or God or the Divine is giving that idea to you as a gift. You didn't ask for it, you didn't prepare yourself for it, but there it is, coming into your awareness. It came to you as a gift. It came by grace. You are honoring the idea when you take action on it. There's a certain blessing that comes with it when you do so. For one thing, the first person to act on an idea is usually the one to profit from it the most.

My rule of thumb is that the universe or God or the Divine gives an idea to more than one person at a time. Why? Because the universe has already learned that not everybody comes from the abundance paradigm. Most people come from the skeptical, scarcity mindset that says, "Oh, the idea is probably is coming to a lot of people," or "I'll get around to it at some other point." The universe, knowing that, gives the idea to five or six or a dozen people all at the same time, knowing most of them won't act on it.

That's the wonderful news for you. The message is for you to act on the idea when you get it, because then the universe is behind you, and, again, you have the energy that comes with the idea to actually get it done.

This is the first take it to the bank tip that I want to give you. When the next idea comes to you, write it down and take action on it. Notice you have good feelings that come with the idea. Use those good feelings to help you manifest the idea. Also, believe that the idea has come to you as a gift and honor it.

The other little secret is that the more you act on your ideas, the more ideas you will get. That's how I've gone from writing one book to writing fifty-three, with more coming. That's how I've gone from not having any audio programs to having several. That's how I've gone from having no DVDs to having many. When the idea comes, I take action. I give thanks for it. The universe acknowledges me by giving me more ideas. I take action on those ideas too, and before you know it, I have an entire career and product line.

This isn't so much about creating a product, it's about living a different kind of life. The life you've had up to now may have been one of scarcity and unhappiness, of struggle and strife. I'm taking you to the abundance paradigm, where life is an escalator ride, where magic and miracles become the norm.

Here is my core message: you could be enlightened and awakened right now if you could be here right now, but you aren't. Most of us aren't. We have worries. We have limiting beliefs. We have negativity. We have memories. We have programming. We have past, present, and future thoughts. All of these things keep us from this moment.

When you get clear of all of those things, when you detach yourself from those thoughts, from those limitations, when you clear up all of the data, when you cleanse yourself of all the programming, you are free to be here now. When you are in this moment, all is well. When you are in this moment, you see magic and miracles everywhere you turn. When you are in this moment, the law of attraction and the law of creation happen naturally. You no longer think about it. You breathe it. When you are in this moment, you live the abundance paradigm. That's what's in this moment, and that's what awaits you.

When I talk about the abundance paradigm, I'm talking about a way for you to understand life in a way that makes sense. One of my favorite authors is Dr. David Hawkins. He has a map of consciousness that helps explain many things in our lives. For example, a person who feels shame, guilt, apathy, grief, or fear is coming from a very low level of consciousness. In the abundance paradigm, we want to come from a very high level of awakening. These stages of enlightenment, peace, joy, love, reason, acceptance are from a much higher level of consciousness.

The abundance paradigm is all-encompassing in the sense that if you are feeling angry or resentful, you have to realize that you're coming from a lower level of awakening. In many ways, it's not awakening at all. But if you're aware of what's going on, on some level you are awakening. You want to come from love. You want to come from bliss. You want to come from serenity. As you do, you move in the direction of the abundance paradigm.

Think about the different levels of emotion, and consider which level are you on right now. If you are on a lower level, that doesn't mean anything bad. You're not to blame. But you are responsible for being at that level, and as you go through the processes I will discuss here, you will transcend it. For now, just note that observation; bookmark it. That's where you are at the moment. As you love yourself at that level, as you forgive it, you will go up the map of consciousness. You will go up through the stages of awakening toward the abundance paradigm shift.

Let me give you another thought. A lot of people are worried about money, and worry about money is coming from the scarcity mindset. Obviously, it's a lower level of consciousness. If you want to come from an abundance paradigm, what thought would you have about money? The one that I like is from an author by the name of Arnold Patent, who said, "The sole purpose of money is to express appreciation."

When I first heard that, it made my mind stop. I thought, "What does he mean? The only purpose of money is to show gratitude, to show appreciation. Does that make any sense?" When I first looked at this idea, I realized that I was looking at it from a scarcity mindset, from the old-school way of understanding money.

From the perspective of the abundance paradigm, money is actually nothing but energy, a very high energy. The higher your energy, the more you'll be able to bring in higher amounts of money. The sole purpose of money is to express appreciation. When you're paying a bill, instead of grumbling about it, say thank you for the fact that you're able to pay for that item. When you're buying anything, feel appreciation. Appreciation is on a higher level on the map of consciousness, and it's going to take you in the direction of the abundance paradigm.

Whenever you think of money, think of it as a beloved tool. As you pay your bills, write checks, or do any spending, investing, giving, or sharing with money, consider its sole purpose to be a means of expressing appreciation. As you do it, feel that appreciation. From the standpoint of the law of attraction, the more you feel appreciation, the more you will attract things to appreciate. Your moments will become more enriched as you appreciate this moment. And the more you take action in terms of investing, spending, and giving money, following your inspiration, the more you engage the law of attraction. Combine the law of attraction and the law of creation to move toward the abundance paradigm.

Let me address something else that may be on your mind. Throughout your life, there are going to be rough patches. There is an up and down that's called the roller coaster of life, as well as the roller coaster of the economy. Sometimes it's going to be rosy, and sometimes it's going to be bleak. How do you live the abundance paradigm when you can't predict the future, when you don't know what your life, the country's life, or the economy's life is going to be like?

This is where you have to trust. Trust is another viewpoint that comes from higher consciousness, and it's essential to the abundance paradigm. You have to trust in the Divine, in yourself, in the process of life.

Decades ago, I heard that life is just a roller coaster. If you can stay in your seat, buckle your seat belt, and go for the ride, you can enjoy it. You can enjoy the ups as well as the downs. The more you enjoy every moment, the more you will attract abundance to you, no matter what is going on in the economy, in the country, in the political system, or even in your personal life. You can transform your situation with the law of creation and the law of attraction. You can live from the abundance paradigm. When you do, things will come to you in such a way that other people will be scratching their heads, wondering how you did it.

In the United States, we went through the Great Depression, which started in 1929. We've actually gone through seventeen recessions in our history. We've lived through all of them. The country goes on, people go on, the economy goes on. There will always be ups and downs.

If you get attached to the ups and downs, if you get attached to worry and struggle, you're actually going to be attracting these things. You will be attracting more scarcity. You'll be attracting more concern. When you move into the abundance paradigm, you start appreciating everything. You start taking action on your ideas. You can be immune to the outside sources.

You have an internal power that is separate from what's going on with the story that's unfolding in the world. No matter what's going on with the economy, you can be immune to it. No matter what's going on with the country, you can still prosper. No matter what's going on with your family and friends, you can be the pillar of strength who knows the secret to the abundance paradigm.

If you want the world to be a happier, healthier, wealthier place, contribute a happy, healthy, wealthy person to it—you. Focus on yourself. Focus on your well-being. Focus on becoming a living, breathing abundance paradigm. Then you can attract the riches that you can use to help your family, friends, your community, the country.

I'm at a point now where I'm doing such things as starting Operation Yes. Operation Yes is my movement to end homelessness in America. How am I able to do this? Because I've mastered the abundance paradigm.

Although the rest of the world might be worried about money, I know how to attract it, and I'm teaching you how to do it in this book.

Learn the law of attraction as I'm teaching it here. Learn the law of creation as I'm teaching it here. Become the abundance paradigm, and you can be the person who withstands everything else going on around them; you can be free.

Let me give you some practical things to do to keep your energy and vibration up and to lead you toward an abundance paradigm shift. These are things anybody can do—including you right this moment.

The first one is, *feel gratitude*. What does that mean? Look around in this moment, and honestly find something you are grateful for. It could be this book. It could be somebody in your house. It could be a pet, a loved one, or your job. It could be something in your immediate environment. Look around, and honestly find something your grateful for, and get into the experience of gratitude.

Gratitude in itself is the number one way to change your life from the inside out in this moment. Believe me: when you start practicing gratitude, your next moments become better, because from the standpoint of the law of attraction, you attract what you're currently feeling. As you're feeling this gratitude, you will attract more to be grateful for.

Do this. Don't just think about it. Do it right now. Look around. What are you grateful for? Say it out loud. Feel it. Get into the feeling.

Another thing you can do right now is *smile*. Don't think that this is too simple or inexpensive. It will transform your consciousness. A lot of the new science going on about understanding the brain says that just by smiling, you will change your energy field and your energy system.

You don't even need a reason to smile. When you say the world *smile*, smile. When you think about smiling, smile. When you think of this book, smile. Think of something in your life that makes you smile or even laugh. Go ahead and do it.

The next thing you can do is to *raise your vibration*. The higher your vibration, the faster you're going to get the results that you're trying to attract in your life.

The next thing you can do is *laugh*. You can laugh from hearing a great joke, or from understanding something that you hadn't understood. You can remember something that somebody told you a long time ago and just laugh.

You don't even need a reason to laugh. You can use it as a meditation. There were actually groups of people out there who get together, and they just laugh. They sit around and start laughing uproariously, for no reason at all. As they start laughing, they laugh even more.

You can do the *up thinking* that I've already mentioned. Whenever negative thoughts come up, let them serve as an alarm system in your head. As soon as you start to have a negative thought and you realize it—you're worried about your job, about the economy, about the bills—stop and turn it around right there. Do what-if-up thinking. Ask yourself questions like, what if it works out? What if I get a better job? What if the bills are paid? What if something wonderful happens? What if the next moment is great? Turn those thoughts around. Do up-spiral thinking.

Another thing you can do is *turn off the news*. I've talked to many people who have been very successful despite the economic ebbs and flows of life. These things are always changing, but if you turn off the news, as these people have done, you'll found you're no longer being programmed in a negative way.

The media is programming you to think in terms of lack and limitation. The programming on television and most of the media is not about abundance. It is about pain. It is about scarcity. It is about a lower level of consciousness.

You want to come from abundance. In order to do that, turn off the news. Be very selective about what you're paying attention to. You don't need to know what's going on in another country, in another economic or political system. Focus on your life, and make a difference in it. Turn off the news.

You can also start *reading success literature*. Read my books and other books in the same category. Go to the self-help section of the bookstore. Read the books that make you feel better, that enrich you.

You've already been brainwashed in a negative way, in a scarcity way. Brainwash yourself in a positive way, in an abundant way. Handpick the biographies you want to listen to or read— biographies of people that have inspired you. Read their stories, learn from their lessons, and keep feeding your mind this positive material. Listen to positive, uplifting audios. All of this material will change your life.

At this point, let me give you a few thought-provoking questions that summarize the ideas in this chapter:

What is a paradigm?

What is a scarcity mindset?

What is an abundance paradigm?

What paradigm are you living from right now?

Can you predict your next thought?

What can you do to change thoughts that arise that you don't care for?

What is the best way to create something new? What is the law of attraction?

What is the law of creation?

When you are in this moment, what occurs for you?

What is the sole purpose of money?

What is your favorite way to raise your vibration?

As we continue on our journey with the abundance paradigm, I'm going to be leading you through some powerful, in-depth exercises designed to clear and cleanse you of the negativity of your previous paradigm. They will help you get clear so you can experience the abundance paradigm as a new way of living.

I'm going to be teaching you some advanced clearing techniques. They're not scary, nor do you have to have any previous preparation for them, but they are new material. I'll walk you through. I'll take you by the hand. I'll carefully, gently guide you through them. On the other side is a world of magic and miracles that you'll be able to experience on a moment by moment basis.

Let me walk you through these cleaning and clearing processes. Let me help you get clear. Let me take you to the next level. Let me help you live the abundance paradigm.

2

The Whiteboard Meditation

In this session, I'm going to walk you through a new clearing exercise called the *whiteboard meditation*. It's been tested in my life, and I have tested it in public sessions. It's a very powerful cleansing tool, and it takes you to the essence of the abundance paradigm. It takes you to that place that we'll call *Source*, where abundance actually comes into being.

I'm talking about the place beyond thought—behind thought. I've often asked people to imagine their thoughts and then pay attention to the fact that they can watch their thoughts, which means that they are not their thoughts; they're separate from these thoughts. This is a very important insight, which enables us to go closer to where the abundance paradigm becomes a new way of living and being.

I advise people to pay attention to their feelings. You notice you have feelings, but again, you're not necessarily your feelings. You can observe them. When you do, you realize you're actually separate from them.

I also invite people to be aware of their body. How does it feel? Are they sitting? Are they standing? Are they moving? Are they exercising? Are they relaxing? Are they lying down? What's the body feel like? You are noting how your body feels to you.

If a part of you is separate from your thoughts, from your feelings, and from your body, what is the part that's observing all of these things?

As I walk you through this exercise, it's perfectly fine to relax if you want to. You can leave your eyes open; you can leave your eyes closed—whatever feels best for you in the situation.

As you are living and breathing, note that you are separate from your thoughts. They're coming and going. They're like birds flying across your consciousness, and you're observing them. What is the background to the thoughts? As you're observing the feelings, what is the background that's observing those feelings? As you're feeling your body, observing your body, what is the background that's doing all of that observing?

Some spiritual traditions call this the *witness*. I call it the *whiteboard*, and I do this for a reason. At the very core of life, where the abundance paradigm is a way of being, there are no thoughts, there are no feelings; there is nothing but emptiness.

This emptiness is alive. If there's any word to describe it, it might be *love*, but even *love* is a word we end up writing on the whiteboard of consciousness. As soon as we write a word on it, we've started to separate from the abundance paradigm.

Not long ago, I gave a presentation to a couple hundred people, who were all peers of mine. I put a clean whiteboard on stage, with nothing written on it. You can probably imagine that right now: a whiteboard on a stand with not a word, not a note written on it.

I invited the people in the audience to tell me about all the personal growth methods they knew of. As they came up with them, we wrote them on the whiteboard. There was everything from belief work to breathing, hypnosis, neurolinguistic programming (NLP), affirmations, and visualization.

The list went on and on. We kept writing on the whiteboard until it became almost black with all the words. More personal development methods kept coming up, and I said, "Just keep writing them on the whiteboard, even if you have to write over what's already there."

Sure enough, within only a few minutes, the whiteboard was gone. I looked at the audience and said, "What happened to the whiteboard? Where is it?"

The audience realized that all of the techniques that they had written down on the whiteboard were actually keeping them separate from the whiteboard.

Then I explained to them the process of clearing and cleaning. I said, "All of these techniques are useful at some time and place. The mistake we make is thinking that the same technique is going to be useful and helpful every time we need it."

That may not be the case. It may end up separating us in this moment from the Divinity represented by the whiteboard.

As I explained these points, I started to erase some of the words on the whiteboard so that you could begin to see little patches of white again. I went on to explain that the different techniques we use came as inspiration—meaning that the person who received the idea in that moment most likely received it from the Divine. That was a beneficial, useful idea, and it served its purpose right then and there. But to think that the same idea is going to help every single person on the planet every time it is utilized is a limitation. I went on to explain that the wiser approach is to realize that the more you can clear and cleanse yourself of the negativity and limitations that are in you in this moment, and the more you can let the whiteboard be white, the more inspiration can direct you in what to do next.

As I kept explaining, I kept erasing. People would ask things like, "What's the difference between an intention and an inspiration?" We would go back and forth, looking at the whiteboard, which was still covered with all of these words, with only patches of white showing through. I would say, "Intentions too often come from our ego. We're sitting there and thinking, 'I want to have so much money'; 'I want to have the biggest house'; 'I want to have the biggest business'; 'I want to have the most romantic relationship'; or 'I want to have a particular person.' That's all coming from our ego.

"In the early stages of awakening, our ego is more or less running our lives, and that's pretty much the answer to why our lives don't always work. When we let go of those ego intentions and start allowing divine or inspired intentions to come through, our life begins to shift into an abundance paradigm."

As I explained this, I erased a few more other words from the whiteboard, and you could see a little bit more of the white. I kept pointing out that in the second and third stages of awakening, the ego believes it's in control. In the third stage, it's starting to surrender, but it's still alive and well; in many ways, it's kicking and screaming as it surrenders to the Divine.

We want to go to the whiteboard itself. We want to be inspired by the whiteboard. We want to be inspired by love, by Divinity, by God, breathing through us, living through us.

As I explained these principles, I erased even more of the whiteboard. Then I went on to explain the story of zero limits, of how I learned *ho'oponopono*. Ho'oponopono is a Hawaiian healing technique that I learned many years ago, and I've discussed it in other contexts. I learned it because of a therapist who worked at a mental hospital for the criminally insane. He used the method to help heal an entire ward of mentally ill criminals.

What did he do? As he looked at their charts, he would feel something. He would feel repulsion, anger, sadness, or embarrassment. Whatever he felt, he would clean on—meaning that he would look at the beliefs coming up in him and then erase them in his consciousness, because he was trying to get back to the whiteboard of being in him.

As he was doing this cleaning within him, a miracle took place. Those mentally ill criminals started to get better. These were patients who previously had been so dangerous and violent that they had to be sedated or shackled. This therapist started practicing ho'oponopono, working on himself to erase all of the data, all of the limiting beliefs in him that were keeping him from the whiteboard experience. As he cleansed himself, those patients got better.

As I was explaining this whole story, I kept erasing the whiteboard. As I did, the people in the audience started to realize that the whiteboard was the source of abundance. It was and is the source of inspiration. The whiteboard is the Divinity that we're longing for. It is behind your thoughts, behind your feelings, behind your body awareness right now.

Now as you go through this experience, realize that you are working on two levels: your conscious mind and your unconscious.

Visualize a whiteboard, with thoughts being written on it. Thoughts that are occurring to you right now, maybe skeptical thoughts, maybe loving thoughts, maybe unhappy thoughts, maybe happy thoughts. They are being written on the whiteboard as they come up.

Now, just as you can easily imagine those words being written, I want you to easily imagine them being erased from the whiteboard of your being.

If you're wondering where is this going or how was this working, realize that those are all thoughts from your ego. They are all being written on the whiteboard as you think them. The more you think these thoughts, the more you stay away from this moment.

Again, pick up an eraser in your mind, and start erasing the whiteboard.

I continued to do that with the audience I was teaching. As I did, the whiteboard became clearer and clearer.

All of the words we had written on it were disappearing. We were erasing them. People also realized that these thoughts were being erased from the inside. All of the limitations, the negativity, the beliefs that were keeping them from the whiteboard, keeping them from Divinity, from inspiration, from God, were being erased so they could be here now.

As I looked out over these people, I saw that many of them had tears in their eyes and smiles on their faces. They were being moved in the deepest and most unexpected way—all from realizing that the source of being, the source of the abundance paradigm, is discovered through this simple little visualization. The more they could move towards the whiteboard, the happier they became. The more they could become the whiteboard, the happier they could be all the time.

The whiteboard is an image you can take with you. As you go about your day, if there's a stress, an alarm, a thought you don't like, you can just say, "That's written on the whiteboard. I am detached from the thought. I am detached from the feeling. The whiteboard is the essence, and at essence, I *am* the whiteboard."

Reflect on that image. As you go through this process, relax. You are awake; you are alert. You can close your eyes if you like, but you are awake. There is a relaxed alertness to you. You're alert to the image of a whiteboard behind everything in your life experience. If anything shows up—a memory, a story, an image, a word, a phrase—whether you like it or not, it's bubbling up from your unconscious mind because it's ready to be let go. You don't have to attach to anything. Right now, allow whatever words and images come up for you to be there. Bring up your eraser, and erase them as you do your best to focus on the whiteboard—a plain, bright whiteboard.

This whiteboard meditation is probably far more powerful, dramatic, and advanced than any other technique you've ever come across in your life. While many meditations are superficial, working only on the top level of awareness, this one goes to the core. It's going to the source.

We're talking about the abundance paradigm, and at zero, at the whiteboard, there is nothing but abundance; there is the totality of all possibility.

As you come out of this particular meditation, I'd like to have you consider this: if at the level of the whiteboard, there are no limitations, what will you do? If at the whiteboard, there are no rules, no ceilings to possibilities, who will you be? If at the whiteboard, you are the Divine itself, what does the Divine inspire you to do next?

I strongly suggest that you make notes of your answers. Go to your journal or notebook and write out what this experience was like for you. Note down your feelings, note down anything that occurred for you as an insight.

Finally, I encourage you to always remember the whiteboard as a trigger image. As you go throughout your day, no matter what's going on from time to time, just think of the whiteboard. Let that be a keyword that conjures up the state of detachment. The whiteboard is a trigger to bring you back to the abundance paradigm. From the abundance paradigm, there is no lack. There's no limitation. There's no scarcity. There's unlimited possibility, unlimited potential, and unlimited love. All you have to remember is the whiteboard.

Next I'm going to take you on a hypnotic storytelling experience from the trance of limitation to the trance of abundance. You can do this visualization as you read along, you can do it while having someone read it aloud to you, or you can record yourself reading the instructions and do the meditation while playing it back. It doesn't really matter whether you leave your eyes open or not, but it does matter that you totally relax and go with the storytelling experience.

Your phone should be turned off. You should be guaranteed to have no interruptions.

This process is designed to cleanse and clear you on a very deep, unconscious level. Just trust the process and allow yourself to move into the abundance paradigm.

First of all, take a deep breath, and then let it out slowly. There's no place for you to go, nothing for you to do. Stretch a little bit: stretch your back, stretch your arms, stretch your legs, get into your body. Allow yourself to be here now, and make this your time to relax, to heal, to feel love.

Again, take a deep breath in. Hold it for a second before letting it go in a big sigh. It feels good to relax. You might want to start at your feet, and relax your toe. Wiggle your toes as you relax them and just consciously think, *relaxed.*

You're breathing deeply and evenly, letting go of any concerns and stresses. There's nothing for you to do now except let go. Whenever you feel like it, you can move to the bottom of your feet and relax them; just say *relax* to your feet.

Again, breathing deeply and evenly, you're going to move up your body, going up to your ankles. Wiggle your feet, and make sure that they're relaxing and understanding that you're requesting that they let go. Do the same with your ankles, coming up slowly with this wave of relaxation. A type of love, the wave of caring love goes up your legs, relaxing. You might move a little bit in your body as you adjust yourself. Again, your breathing is deep and easy and relaxed. It feels really good to let go.

You're continuing to let the wave of relaxation come up your body, around your waist, your stomach, your back. Be sure that every cell in your body is relaxing; it's just letting go. Yes, it feels good to relax and let go. That wave of relaxation is going up to your spine, it's letting go all through your back, your shoulders. Then through your abdomen, your chest.

Breathing deep, relax and let go. Nothing to do, nothing to think about. You can even go to sleep if you like and let this message penetrate your unconscious mind. Again, you can totally relax, totally let go, even drift into this refreshing sleep. Your arms relax, and so do your wrist and your hands. Oh, it feels so good just to let go and relax.

Of course, your neck is relaxing. You can feel your head loosening on your neck. The back of your head is relaxing, and so are your face, your eyes, your forehead, the top of your head. Everything is relaxing completely, just letting go. You are awash in the sea of love, bathing you, rejuvenating you, renewing you, relaxing you.

Now imagine that there is a swirl of energy opening your chakras very gently—nothing overwhelming, nothing harmful. This is all a low simmer of love, going around your energy system like an aura around your body. It's protecting you. It's awakening you to abundance.

As you relax in gentle comfort in this protection of energy and let go, imagine walking through an open door, a door that takes you to a paradise. This paradise can be whatever you see, whatever you imagine.

What does the perfect world look like to you? You step through this door, and there, on the other side, is probably color, beauty, light, love. Everything you've ever worried about is gone. Every story you ever told yourself about lack and limitation and scarcity is gone. These things do not exist in this new world. In this new world that you're now living and breathing in, the flowers look more colorful. Their aroma seems more beautiful. The sky seems clearer. Your body feels young and strong, radiant and full of power and energy. Your mind feels clear and open and positive.

As you look around, you can see that there's a type of whiteboard that all of this is coming from. There's a whiteboard that is the source, which is bringing abundance of living into your awareness. The home that you've always wanted to be in is right there. You can actually walk right up to it. As you reach for the front door and open it, it's unlocked. Your name is on the door; you step through it, and you see your home: a home that has nothing but love, abundance, brightness, power, and security.

The vibration of this home is very high. As you walk through it, you can feel it energizing you. It's giving you the energized feeling of love. You're soaking up this healing, rejuvenating experience, and you're realizing, "This is my life. This is abundance. This is my home. This world is real."

You walk through your home, and all the things you've ever wanted to manifest or attract through the law of creation or the law of attraction are here. They already exist. Whether it happens to be—a person, a place, a thing—there it is. You can almost wish it into being, and it appears. It's a magical universe. It's the place of abundance. It's the place of magic and miracles, and it's where you now live.

You wander up the stairs of this house. On the second floor, more miracles are awaiting you. There's a guide here who has a message for you about abundance. This guide could be somebody you know or somebody you've never met before, but it's a loving, wise, safe figure. This wise soul takes a moment to give you a message. Pause and relax as you take in that message. Now smile and thank that wise guide, and then walk to another room.

In another room, another guide has another message for you, about your relationships. Take a moment and listen as this guide gives you an abundant thought about relationships. Again, smile and thank—maybe bow to—the guide, and go to another room.

Yes, there's yet another guide there. This guide has a message for you about prosperity, about abundance itself. Listen as this guide delivers the message to you. Again, give thanks, bow, nod, smile, and move to another floor or another room, whatever is appropriate for you.

This is your magic castle. This is your home of abundance. As you move, you find yet another guide, another safe, wise, loving soul who has a message for you about your health. Listen as you hear this message. Again, give thanks, smile, bow, and move on.

You're noticing that there's wisdom here. You're noticing that you can you go to this home, this place of abundance, whenever you want. It is real. It's as real as anything else in your life at this moment.

As you walk around, you step outside, and you're in the garden, where there is another guide with yet another message for you. Let this message be well received. It's for you personally: about your mission in life, living from the abundance paradigm. Listen attentively as the message is given. Again, give thanks, bow, smile, and move away from that last guide.

As you explore the land around this home of abundance, you find that there's a separate building on the property: a small shrine. Go to that shrine. As you approach it, you see it has a glass door. You can't quite see through the door, but you open it up, go inside, and see an altar. There are candles, lights, and incense, and it feels like the holiest place you've ever come across.

There on the altar is a note. You walk over to it, lift it up, and read it. It says, "What do you want? If you can have, do, or be anything, what would you like to have attracted into your life? What would you like to create in your life? What would you like to experience from the abundance paradigm? What do you want?"

You take a moment to reflect, and almost instantly something shows up. You turn that note over and write your request down, knowing that it is going to come true, because you are in the house of manifestation.

After seeing all of your guides and going through this home of abundance, being in this house of manifestation means that whatever you write down is going to come into your reality, so carefully consider what you want. Write it down as clearly as you can, in as few words as you can. When you're done, turn that paper over, and leave it on the altar. You slowly start to back away from the altar, feeling the wonderful feelings in that area, and then you exit.

You start walking back to the house and go through it, maybe seeing your guides again, smiling and nodding at them. Perhaps one of them has one more message for you, and you pause to hear it.

Then you keep walking until you go through the house and exit, retracing your steps so that you can come back to the place where it all began. As you're leaving that area and returning to the here and now, into your body, you notice that you feel different. You know that something has taken place on a very deep level—a healing, a clearing, a cleansing. Your unconscious mind has been erased of data that was limiting you from feeling abundant, being abundant, and living abundance.

You're very conscious that all of this is real. Yes, it took place in the realm of the mind, but all of it is real.

The guides are real. The messages are real. Your request is real, and your request is going to come into reality.

Now slowly come back into your body. Realize that you are here and now, still at peace, still relaxed, still at ease. Wiggle your toes and shake your hands. Open your eyes, and look around the room. Realize that you're totally awake, you are totally here and now, and you feel totally wonderful. You are wide awake here and now, smiling big, breathing deep, feeling great.

As soon as you have a moment that feels inspired, write down in your notebook all the messages you've gotten from your guides. Write down the request you made, which you know is coming into your life. Describe what it was like to live in the house of abundance. Describe what it is like now to live the abundance paradigm. Anchor this moment with your description. Every now and then, close your eyes and relive it. Whenever you feel inspired, come back and repeat this exercise: go through the wonderment of it all again. Every time you do, you'll get a different message from each guide, and you can make a new request. For now, smile, give thanks, feel gratitude, stretch, and be awake.

You can go through this wonderful hypnotic storytelling experience every day. In fact, I encourage you to do it every night before going to sleep. Now why would I say that? Obviously, it helps you relax. Most of us have stressful days, because we haven't quite merged into the abundance paradigm yet. Until we do, one thing to do is listen, destress, let go of everything that's been going on during the day, focus on what you want, and get into the place where magic and miracles can take place.

Every time you do this exercise, you're going to hear different suggestions from your guides, who are coming from your higher self, your unconscious mind. You're in such a deep state of relaxation that when you place a request, it's like giving an order to the universe. Be very conscious of what you're asking for, because it will come into your reality.

I've been practicing hypnosis since I was sixteen years old. I am a certified hypnotherapist. I have done hypnotic work with dozens and maybe hundreds of people. I have worked with different seminars, the National Guild of Hypnotists, and many other sources. I am a student of Milton Erickson, the famous hypnotist who specialized in story hypnosis. I've used all of these different elements, which I've learned from my experience and education, to create this unique storytelling experience for you.

It's designed to help you relax and drop unconscious defenses and negativity so that we can address the unconscious mind.

Your unconscious mind is far more powerful than your conscious mind. Your conscious mind is aware of about forty bits of information in any one moment, whereas your unconscious mind is aware of about eleven million bits. The unconscious mind is where all of the beliefs, the data, the programming are stored, and it's where you need to do the cleaning and clearing.

This particular trance inducing state, using the story I've just described, is designed to speak to your unconscious mind and help you clear away the debris there so you can live the abundance paradigm. Go through it every day. Go through it whenever you feel inspired to do so, particularly whenever you feel you've been knocked off-center and you feel things aren't going your way.

As I close this chapter, here are some thought-provoking questions that have come from the students in my Miracles Coaching Program. You'll find that they are very deep, very sincere, and very raw, because they're coming from the hearts of people who are feeling these questions.

You may find that as you go back through this book and review the questions again later, your answers may change, because as you go through the process of awakening, you'll get to the place where you are an awakened human being living the abundance paradigm. At that point, your answers are going to be completely different than when you answered them at the first, second, or third level of awakening.

Answer these questions right now. Have fun with them; then come back to them another time and revisit them. This will help you take this process to a whole new level.

- Once I am cleared of major blocks, does inspiration naturally flow to my consciousness, or are other steps necessary?
- What is the difference between inspiration and regular thoughts?
- How can I foster further inspiration once I have received it?
- Why do blocks keep inspiration from happening?
- When I follow inspiration, will I still get resistance?
- Can we be inspired to do something that may not be best for us or that can even hurt us?
- Once I am inspired to do something, how can I keep myself from getting in the way or sabotaging my own success?
- Once the door of inspiration opens up, will it close if I don't act immediately?

We'll continue with more in the next chapter.

3

Clearing with Ho'oponopono

In this chapter, I want to talk to you about the ho'opo-nopono clearing technique. Whether you've heard of it before or not, I'm going to take you to new levels of under-standing. I'll start with the basic method of using ho'opo-nopono to cleanse and clear yourself. Then I'll take you into an advanced method, which you've probably never come across before.

First of all, what is ho'oponopono? Well, that odd sounding word (which you don't have to memorize or know how to spell) refers to a Hawaiian healing tech-nique. At one time, it was secret, but in my audio programs, like *The Secret to Attracting Money* and *The Missing Secret*, I've introduced ho'oponopono to a whole world of people, who have been practicing it by the thousands. These people have been having life changing experiences from this simple technique.

First of all, let me tell you how I discovered this process. As I've already mentioned, years ago a friend of mine heard an incredible story about a therapist who worked in the state hospital for the criminally insane in Hawaii. The people there were criminals, and they were mentally ill. They were put in that institution and locked away. Most of those patients had to be either sedated or shackled, because they were truly dangerous; they were violent. The hospital kept losing staff. Nurses didn't want to be there, doctors didn't want to be there, therapists didn't want to be there.

The hospital was desperate. In their search for somebody to help them, they found an unusual therapist. As the story was told to me, this therapist went to this institution, and he practiced the secret Hawaiian healing technique. As he practiced it, those patients, those mentally ill criminals, started to get better.

This sounds amazing, incredible, miraculous. When I first heard it, I felt disbelief: how in the world could a therapist heal mentally ill criminals? Well, it gets even better, because he helped heal them without even talking to them directly. He didn't touch them. He didn't work with them. He didn't see them in a doctor-client relationship.

This sounded even stranger to me, and I wanted to know the truth. The person who had told me the story only had a vague idea about it. I thought it was an urban legend; I thought it had to be fiction. I went on a quest to find the therapist, the hospital, and the people who were there. I ended up writing an entire book called *Zero Limits*, which tells the whole story.

The therapist is named Dr. Ihaleakala Hew Len. I call him Dr. Hew Len. He and I became friends.

I first found him by phone. I got on the phone with him and asked him all about the hospital story. He said it was true.

"But what were you doing to heal these people?" I asked.

"I was simply cleaning and clearing myself."

That made no sense to me, and I asked him to explain. He said he was using a method that he called ho'oponopono. I didn't know how to spell it; I didn't know how to pronounce it; I wasn't about to remember it. At that point, it was too confusing.

Dr. Hew Len went on to say that a kahuna, a Hawaiian mystery teacher, had taught this technique to him, and he'd been practicing it for twenty-five years. When the hospital hired him to come in and work with those patients, the administrators were desperate. They said, "We just need a therapist on staff. You can do whatever you want, but in order for us to get our funding, we need to have a certified mental health practitioner working for the hospital."

Dr. Hew Len made this agreement whereby he would sit in his office and look at the patient's files. As he looked at their files, he practiced this basic Hawaiian healing technique on himself. As he practiced it on himself, those patients started to get better.

I was probably just as confused as you might be, and I kept asking, "How does this work?"

Dr. Hew Len explained that we create everything in our lives. We are 100 percent responsible for everything that shows up. There are no exceptions. There are no loopholes. There's no get-out-of-jail card.

As I continued to talk to Dr. Hew Len, he asked, "Have you ever heard the phrase, you create your own reality?"

"Of course. I write about that; I teach it." *You create your own reality* is a kind of mantra with people in the self-help and personal transformation movement.

Dr. Hew Len went on to stretch my mind in such a way that's it's never gone back to its previous shape. He went on to say, "If you create your own reality, and a mentally ill criminal shows up in it, didn't you also create that person?"

He was saying that 100 percent responsibility means everything, everybody, every incident that shows up in your life, whether you like it or not—good, bad, indifferent, however you have been judging it—you have created. You brought it into your life.

This is a quantum jump in understanding personal responsibility. A person once told me, "This isn't 100 percent responsibility, this is 200 percent responsibility, because you're taking on the responsibility of what seem to be the other people who show up in your life."

Dr. Hew Len went on to explain that he took responsibility for everything that was showing up. Since these patients showed up in his life because he was now working at that hospital, he had to take responsibility for them. How did he do that? He realized that because of the law of attraction, deep inside of him, maybe and most likely unconsciously, there was a magnetic force that put him and them in the same place.

This force put these people together for a reason: because of programming. This programming is largely in the dark corners of our mind. We're not even aware it's there. You look around and ask, "Why did this person show up in my life?" or, "Why did this experience happen?" or, "Why did this bad thing happen?" You did cocreate it, you did attract it, but you didn't do it knowingly or consciously, any more than Dr. Hew Len consciously created those patients. Unconsciously, there's a whole lot of programming going on.

Dr. Hew Len went on to say that that programming inside of him, which cocreated all of those patients who showed up in his life, had to be cleaned. That programming, those limitations, those beliefs were in his unconscious. They were causing these things to show up in his life, and they had to be washed away. He did that with ho'oponopono. How? He went on to say that all he was here to do was clean and clear.

"What does that mean?" I asked.

"Joe, even as I'm talking to you right now, all I'm doing is cleaning and clearing. What I did with those mentally ill patients was clean and clear."

"What does that mean?"

"All I am doing is having a conversation inside of myself with Divinity, with God"—with the whiteboard. "I'm simply saying four phrases as a kind of mantra, as a kind of psalm, as a kind of prayer."

These were the four phrases:

I'm sorry.

Please forgive me.

Thank you.

I love you.

When he told me those phrases, again it didn't make sense. I wondered, "How do those four phrases erase the programming that's in your unconscious mind and attracting these experiences?"

If you really want to shift into the abundance paradigm, you have to clean up the old paradigm. Dr. Hew Len's method is a terrific way to do it. All you do is silently, inside of yourself, think of whatever is concerning you—whether it's another person, a problem, a situation, or whatever it happens to be—and then consider your relationship to what I call the whiteboard. Consider your relationship to God, to Spirit—whatever the word is for you—and speak those four phrases to your connection to Spirit: *I'm sorry, please forgive me, thank you,* and *I love you.* Dr. Hew Len says, "Say them in whatever order you like. It doesn't matter at all."

Why are you saying these particular phrases? Here's how I explain it. Of course, I've been doing this for years now. Dr. Hew Len and I have done several seminars together, and he's been to my home, and we coauthored the book *Zero Limits.* I've gotten to be very much inside the mind of Dr. Hew Len.

I practice ho'oponopono by saying, "Please forgive me, because I have been unaware. Please forgive me, because I did not know what the unconscious programming inside of myself was. I'm sorry that I was asleep. I'm sorry that I was unconscious. I'm sorry that I wasn't aware of the programming, wherever it came from. Please forgive me for not being aware. I'm sorry for being unconscious."

Then I move into *thank you,* because a statement of gratitude, as I've already said, is one of the most powerful ways to move yourself into the abundance paradigm of this moment. By saying *thank you,* you start to move in the direction of gratitude. As you say *thank you,* you start to feel different within yourself. This new feeling is going to engage the law of attraction in a very positive way. You'll start to attract more of what you want in your life. More importantly, you're saying *thank you* to Divinity. You're saying *thank you* to the whiteboard, to God, for handling this issue for you, for handling and erasing this problem.

I like to end with *I love you* because I think the essence of God, of Spirit, of the whiteboard, is love. As soon as I say *I love you*, I start to move in the direction of being one with God, with the whiteboard. The more you can feel love, the closer you will be to having the abundance paradigm as a permanent way of being in your life.

I'm sorry, please forgive me, thank you, I love you: those are the four phrases Dr. Hew Len has been saying. He says he does them all the time.

"Right now," I asked, "as I'm talking to you, are you doing them?"

"Yes. I've learned that as I'm talking to people, as I'm talking to even you right now, in the back of my mind that new self-talk is going on. I'm saying *I'm sorry, please forgive me, thank you, I love you*, silently in my mind as a healing technique."

As I write this book, I am healing anything between you and me, being in this moment and experiencing the abundance paradigm that's right now. I'm cleaning and clearing, so I can be here now, so there is no negativity in me as I write this book for you. I'm doing this because you are a mirror of me. The cleaner and clearer I can be within me, the cleaner and clearer you can be in your everyday reality.

That's the basic ho'oponopono technique. Again, it's simply those four phrases: *I'm sorry, please forgive me, thank you,* and *I love you.*

Some people don't like to say *I'm sorry* or *please forgive me.* They don't feel comfortable with these statements. I remember the first person who told me that. It shocked me, and I wondered why they wouldn't say *I'm sorry* or *please forgive me.*

Then it occurred to me: from an ego standpoint, we never want to know that we've been wrong. We always want to think we're in the right. At the first stage of awakening, the stage of victimhood, you believe that it's always the other people who did things wrong; it's never you. In order to awaken, to shift into the abundance paradigm, you're going to have to take 100 percent responsibility for your life.

If you have problems saying *I'm sorry* or *please forgive me*, you have a couple of options. You can omit those two statements. You really don't have to say them. In fact, many times all you have to say is *I love you.* If you just walk around saying *I love you* in your mind, you will change your energy and energy field, and you'll interact with everybody completely differently.

Imagine if eight billion people on the planet were walking around saying *I love you* in their minds. Their entire lives would be different. This planet would be different.

If you only want to say two basic phrases, say, *I love you* and *thank you.* You can skip those two: *please forgive me* and *I'm sorry.* But my stronger advice is to use all four phrases on your resistance to saying *I'm sorry.*

In other words, whatever shows up in your world, whether it is another person that you're not getting along with, a situation you're not feeling comfortable with, some sort of longstanding problem, or even the resistance to saying these four phrases—use the four phrases on them.

This is the basic ho'oponopono method. Try it now. Relax and let something come into your mind that you want to clear on. If you don't have anything, still say the phrases and trust that you're cleaning and clearing unconscious programming of which you're not even aware.

I'm sorry. Please forgive me. Thank you. I love you. Say them for as long as feels right to you.

I want to go on to describe an advanced ho'oponopono clearing technique. This is not in any of my other books; I've not written about it; nor has Dr. Hew Len. It's something that was taught to me privately in person by Dr. Hew Len. He has been a type of shaman or guru in my life. He is a person who lives in the abundance paradigm.

One time, Dr. Hew Len came into Austin, Texas, where I was living at the time. I picked him up at the airport. For some reason the bags were very late—thirty or forty minutes late. Dr. Hew Len and I were standing there at the terminal, waiting for the baggage to come down.

I always use every moment I have with Dr. Hew Len to pick his brains and find out what he's doing next and what's in his heart. I was telling him about a particular issue that was troubling me. It was a longstanding issue in my life, and I was doing everything I could think of to remove it. I was doing the basic cleaning and clearing of ho'oponopono; I was doing it nonstop and intensely, but I felt as if nothing was happening. I was feeling that the situation wasn't unfolding; it wasn't clearing; it wasn't changing.

I was telling Dr. Hew Len all of this. He said, "Here is something you need to remember: as you are cleaning and clearing, you are taking away programming layer by layer that you're not even aware of. All of the programming that's going on in your unconscious mind is so deep and such a huge collection of beliefs that it's a mindset, a paradigm of its own, that is pretty well locked. You have so much cleaning and clearing to do that it may take a while before you see the situation resolved."

I jokingly told Dr. Hew Len, "I'm enough of an entrepreneur to want to know how to instantaneously change.

I want to find the easy button, which I just push to transform my life."

He laughed and said, "Well, there is an advanced way of doing cleaning."

I, of course, almost jumped down his throat because I wanted to know this advanced form of ho'oponopono right then and there. In fact, I wanted to know why I hadn't learned it previously. Maybe I should have realized that this moment was when I needed to know it: all the previous cleaning that I had done—saying *I'm sorry, please forgive me, thank you, I love you*—prepared me for this moment, when I could hear the advanced technique that Dr. Hew Len wanted to teach me. It just happened to take place at an airport baggage station.

As I was standing with him, he said, "Do you have a business card?"

I pulled out a business card. Dr. Hew Len told me that I could use it as a cleaning tool. "You can just swipe it over anything that's bothering you. You can swipe it over your body and make yourself feel better. You can write down the name of a person or place or thing that's bothering you, and you can swipe or rub your card over it, and the situation will get better."

I already knew that technique and had already practiced it, but the advanced one was still to come. I pulled out my business card, and I showed it to Dr. Hew Len.

He went on to say, "Imagine the energy behind the problem that you're complaining about. Take your business card, and in your mind, take the edge of it, and pretend it's like a knife or a pair of scissors. You're going to slice through the energy of that visualization."

I raised up my business card and pretended that that energy field was right in front of me, like a thought form in the air. Then I pretended that I was cutting it up. As I cut it up, it seemed to disappear.

Keep in mind that there was nobody else in front of me. The problem wasn't in front of me. My perception of the problem was in front of me, and it was very real, because I could feel it. As I was feeling it, I cut it up with my business card. As I cut it up with my business card, slicing it left and right and up and down, it dissolved into energy, into matter, into dust, and left. I felt it leave my body. I felt the situation was resolved, and I knew on some level that that had actually taken place.

Now of course the luggage came at that point, because synchronicity was at work: everything we needed to tell each other was done. We were able to go about our day, so we got the luggage and left.

I kept this advanced technique to myself. I didn't share it with other people because I thought they might not be ready for it or understand it. Besides, I knew the basic ho'oponopono method was pretty powerful all by itself. As long as people said, *I'm sorry, please forgive me, thank you, I love you* in their minds to Divinity, they would be evolving, growing, transforming, and getting closer to the abundance paradigm.

A few months passed and I thought, "I'm going to teach this to other people." In one seminar, I stood on stage and started to walk people through this advanced technique. To my amazement, I looked out, and people started crying. They were having breakthroughs as they were doing this simple visualization.

I suppose it's more than visualization, because we're tapping into the energy of the Hawaiian healing system. Dr. Hew Len is a type of shaman from that mystery tradition. What he was passing on to me, and I'm passing on to you, is more than a visualization or mental imagery experience. It actually dislodges the energy causing the problem. With this healing method, you can break free of some of the more stubborn issues in your life.

Let me walk you through this method now. You can do it in any situation or position, but I do want you to be alert. You don't have to close your eyes unless you want to.

Take a deep breath, hold it for a second, and let it out. Relax, let go, and think about a person, situation, or problem that has surfaced in your life. If there are several, just take one. Another possibility is to see if they all have something in common. Maybe you can work on them all because they're all in one category.

For the sake of this advanced ho'oponopono method, allow whatever comes to you to volunteer to be erased. It could be something that's been longstanding. Now it's time for it to be healed.

As this problem comes into your awareness, notice that it is your perception that calls it a problem. In other words, you have labeled this as a problem, whereas other people looking at it may not see it as such. To them, it may simply be a series of facts, a story, without any energy in it whatsoever. Dr. Hew Len has often said, "Have you ever noticed that when there's a problem, you are there?" He means that you are the one creating it, attracting it, and experiencing it.

As you're feeling this truth, realize that you have brought this situation into your awareness for a lesson. You might give yourself a moment to see what the lesson is. Once you get the lesson, you no longer need the experience. If you had to guess what the lesson is in this particular problem, what would you say? Dr. Hew Len has often invited me to trust my intuition, saying there's no right or wrong, but if you just imagine what the answer might be, what comes up?

You have this ball of energy in front of you. You have your perception of it. You might even be feeling it in your body, and it might make you angry or upset. It doesn't matter; whatever you're feeling is OK. In the background of your mind, you might even have the new self-talk going on: *I'm sorry, please forgive me, thank you,* and *I love you.* You're feeling this problem, but you're addressing God or the Divine or the whiteboard, and you're pleading for it to be erased. *I'm sorry, please forgive me, thank you, I love you. I'm sorry, please forgive me, thank you, I love you.*

Now while that energy is there, and you're feeling it, getting the lesson from it, and saying these four phrases of the basic cleaning technique, imagine taking a business card—yours, mine, or somebody else's. It's a small, rectangular piece of cardboard, and the edges of it can be fairly sharp. Raise that business card up in your mind, and bring it down on the ball of energy that represents that problem in front of you, slicing it in half. Then you might raise your hand again and come down to slice it again. You want to do this several times while you break up that energy. Take a moment to really get into breaking up the energy, slicing through it with the business card. As you're doing it, you're saying, *I'm sorry, please forgive me, thank you, I love you.* Do that for a moment or two.

Now take a deep breath and allow the energy field that you're in and in front of you to clear. Let the dust settle. Let the particles fall like stardust. The ball of energy that was in front of you is gone. The problem field is gone. The perception of it as an issue in your life is gone. What remains is a sense of peace, well-being, happiness, and love. This place, where there are no problems, is the abundance paradigm. This place of clarity is the abundance paradigm. This place of healing, of transformation, of rest and recovery, is the abundance paradigm.

Now stretch, make notes of your discoveries, smile, relax, and enjoy the miracle of this moment.

You can use this simple but advanced ho'oponopono technique for anything that may show up in your life. When Dr. Hew Len was working with those mentally ill criminals at the hospital in Hawaii, he said those phrases as he felt all of the issues in him come up when he was looking at the records of those patients. He would simply be saying *I love you, I'm sorry, please forgive me,* and *thank you.*

In any case, I've just given you an advanced technique that handles the most troublesome issues. It's another tool for you to keep in your bag of tricks.

As you go about your day, you want to stay focused in the moment, and you can do that by watching your breathing or by touching a physical object in your environment and reminding yourself that you are here. Another method is to watch your thoughts, realizing that you're not your thoughts; watch your feelings, realizing that you're not your feelings; and feel your inner body, realizing that you're not your body; you're behind all of those things. You are, in essence, the whiteboard.

These techniques help you understand that the whiteboard is not only clean and clear and represents love but is God or Spirit or the Divine, and it is you. From that place, you can live as Divinity, which is the fourth stage of awakening, where the abundance paradigm is now your new way of being.

At this point, you may be wondering what these exercises have to do with the law of attraction and the law of creation. They have everything to do with both.

First of all, we're attracting everything into our lives because of our unconscious beliefs. Obviously, we need to do clearing and cleansing work there to change our unconscious mind, so we get more of the results that we want. That's from the law of attraction standpoint; it should be pretty clear.

What about from the standpoint of the law of creation? Everything that you have happening in your life right now you have not only attracted but created: you cocreated it on an unconscious level.

When you first hear this, you may think, "I didn't create this particular problem; I didn't create this particular person." But in our deeper understanding of how the universe works, you are 100 percent responsible for everything in your life. In a way, as I've already suggested, you are 200 percent responsible: you're creating your life experience from the law of creation, but you're also creating your perception of everybody else's life experiences, again from the law of creation.

Now the law of creation has a lot to do with action. The actions you take click into gear. They are a mechanism that, through the law of attraction, brings everything you're getting into your life. In other words, these two laws are working hand in hand. In order to experience the abundance paradigm, you're going to have to work with both of them.

I'm making it easy. I'm making it almost brainless and effortless. All you have to do is read this book and follow the directions, and the transformation will take place in you. The law of attraction and the law of creation are the two fundamentals at the core of this whole program. They will lead you to what you want: the abundance paradigm mind shift.

4

Beyond Complaint

n this chapter, I'm going to give you the most powerful
cleaning and clearing technique I've ever come up with
in my life. This is one I've personally used, polished, and
refined. It is based on a two-thousand-year-old ritual
from ancient Tibet, which I've experimented with and
updated it for modern times. I'm going to teach you the
Vitale clearing method.

This particular method will help you with the law of
attraction and the law of creation, because it will clear
up how you are attracting people that you're not getting
along with in your life. It will help remedy how you've
been using the law of creation to cocreate people you have

issues with. In other words, the clearer you get in relation-ships with other people, and, more importantly, with your relationship with yourself, and, even more importantly, with your relationship with the Divine, the closer you will get to living the abundance paradigm. If you're trying to live the abundance paradigm but have an issue with another person, you're not going to be happy, relaxed, or whole. You're likely to attract more issues with more people, because you haven't resolved the key issue. You're going to create more blocks on your road to success.

Clear the issue with another person, with yourself, and with the Divine; then you are free to live the abun-dance paradigm. You can do this easily and effortlessly.

This is a very powerful exercise. It goes very deep. It helps you release any core issues with another person.

Be sure that you're home, you're alone, you're safe, the phone, computer, and fax machine are off, and your door is closed. Make sure that you will not be interrupted for the next twenty minutes or so.

Begin by bringing to mind somebody with whom you're having an issue. (I'm on the board of directors of A Complaint Free World, the organization Will Bowen founded after writing his book *A Complaint Free World*. He pointed out all of our complaints in life have to do with other people.) Allow somebody you've been com-plaining about to surface in your awareness.

Somebody you want to clear, cleanse, be at peace with. Take whatever comes into your awareness, whoever that might be. It could be a family member, business partner, somebody in a relationship, or somebody from the past.

Now that you have an image of this person mentally in front of you, don't fight with it, don't argue with it, don't feel repulsed by it. You can allow whatever you're feeling to be there, but you want to come, to the best of your ability, from a place of curiosity.

Ask yourself, what does this person want? Now pretend that the image in front of you is actually the person that you're dealing with. Do your best to visualize this person in front of you as a real, breathing human being in your energy field right now. You can speak to it and ask, "What do you want?"

Allow your awareness of the answers to go very deep. While the image might say something superficial, what do you think the image really wants, deep down in its soul? What does it want from life, from itself, from you? Give yourself a moment to listen to what it wants. You are actually conversing with this image. It is an actual representation of the person with whom you're having an issue.

Pay attention to the image for another moment or two.

Have a dialogue in which you repeatedly ask, "What do you want?" See if the answer changes. More often than not, on a deep level, what a person wants is love. See if the image in front of you says that.

Now I want you to do something that at first will seem a little awkward. You've welcomed the image of this person. You've looked at it with curiosity, and you've wondered what it wants. Then you asked it, "What do you want from me?" You got some sort of answer, which may shed some light on this person's behavior. Maybe you understand that the other person really wants love, recognition, the feeling of acceptance. Again, you're not focused on yourself; you're focused on this image of this person.

The next thing I want you to do is to feed this image from your own body. You imagine that you are taking your body, the flesh of your body, and handing it to this image, you are nourishing it, you are feeding it your own essence. Obviously, this isn't happening in reality, and you're not doing anything to your own body or anybody else's. In this clearing visualization, you're imagining giving the essence of you, your body, your soul, your energy, to this image, to this person.

Just imagine reaching into your own body, scooping up your flesh, handing it to this image, and watching the image eat. You are nourishing this image. You are helping to give it what it really wants. This may seem strange, but trust the process. Nothing is being done to hurt you or anyone else. You are simply visualizing feeding what you once thought was the enemy.

Take a few minutes to feed this image in your mind. Again, you're feeding your body to this image. You're scooping up your flesh, your soul, your bodily energy, and handing it to the image in front of you.

Allow this process to go on for a few minutes. Then finish up feeding the image in front of you. If it seems to want more from you, go ahead and feed it some more. (You can also do this exercise again, or you can continue to do it in your mind even after this session ends.)

As you're finishing up feeding this image, notice that it is now content. You have accepted it, you have looked at it with curiosity, being nonattached to it; you have fed it from your own body. You have loved it; you have listened to it. It feels heard, it feels loved, it feels satisfied. In your mind, you can see this image smile, feel content, and start to disappear. It's leaving your body and mind. It's leaving your energy field. It's leaving you completely. You are free.

You can use this clearing method whenever you have an issue with another person. You simply think of that person and go through the process. There are basically four steps:

1. Visualize the person in front of you, and do so with love and curiosity.
2. Ask what the image what it wants.

3. In this, the longest segment, feed it of your own body, nourish it, give of yourself.
4. Finally, see the image go, to leave your awareness entirely.

Whenever you do this exercise, you'll end up in a place of peace, which will help you create and attract the wonderful experiences you want. It will also release all the stuck energy that's been there in the past; it will release all the issues that have bothered you but you have been unable to let go of.

This powerful technique has been refined to work for today's world, but it is based on ancient mystery school traditions. While it does deal with the visualization of another person, you're really dealing with the energy of your perception of that person. When you clear that energy, the other person more often than not self-corrects or even leaves your life orbit. Either way, you're free. That's the power of this particular clearing method.

Clearing yourself of any and all negativity in your body and mind and unconscious is very relevant to the abundance paradigm, because we need to clear up the nagging beliefs that are hidden from our awareness. You're trying to use the law of attraction—maybe you're already using it and having some success—you're creating your reality using the law of creation, and you're starting to take more action. To streamline your success, accelerate all your results, and actually live the abundance paradigm, you've got to remove all of the negativity in you.

This may end up being a lifelong process, because we are humans becoming awake. The spirituality that's within us is somewhat hidden by the human nature with which we came into the world. We have some work to do, but we can speed up the process by using these technologies, which have been around for centuries.

Now I'm going to give you a chant that is designed to cleanse you and protect you. It protects you from any interference as you are dumping your unconscious programming. There's also programming still trying to attach itself to you. What do you do about that? How do you put up your force field? How do you protect yourself?

I'm going to give you an ancient Indian mantra. It's from the Sanskrit language, and it's designed to clear you of negativity and strengthen your energy system. It's working on two levels. It's going to help you with the law of attraction and of course the law of creation. It works on your unconscious mind to clear out the negativity that's keeping you from the bliss of this moment. It also protect you from any negativity that might be coming from the world, from the media, from other people, that is trying to enter your mind right now. All you have to do is listen to this Sanskrit chant (you can find recordings of it, showing its pronunciation, on YouTube and elsewhere on the Internet). The mantra is:

Om Hanumate namaha

You can relax and listen to this mantra while you are driving, when you go to bed at night, or while you're watching TV. (Of course, turn off the mainstream news.) You can listen to it while you are exercising, or you can have it in the background as you're working at your computer. In fact, I probably would recommend that you put it on and let it play all day long in the background of your life.

If you feel like doing the chant at any point, then just go ahead and chime in. Or you can chant it yourself in any circumstances you happen to find yourself in.

Again, this mantra is going to help engage the law of creation, the law of attraction, and the law of protection. It's going to help you cleanse and protect yourself, and it'll help lead you to the abundance paradigm.

5
Tough Questions

n this chapter, I'm going to answer questions that have
come to me from students in my Miracles Coaching Program. They have been learning about the law of attraction
and the law of creation, and they're trying to apply the
abundance paradigm in their lives. These questions are
from them, not from me, so they're very sincere, they're
very raw, they're very human. They're coming directly
from their soulful, earth-level experience of reality right
now. Some of these questions are blunt, some are tough,
some are rough. But I'm going to answer them, because I
know most of these questions are on your mind as well.

This will help you reinforce and better understand everything we've been talking about and the processes you've been going through so far.

How can you tell the difference between inspiration and your own deep-seated thoughts and wishes?

We have two choices in life: we can come from inspiration, or we can come from programming. Most of us are coming from programming, meaning that we're driven by our unconscious belief system, our old paradigm. We're driven by the beliefs we acquired as we were growing up. This make it very hard for inspiration to come through from the Divine.

When I asked Dr. Hew Len this question, he said, "You can't tell the difference at first." At first, when you're first learning these processes, and you're learning about the law of creation and the law of attraction, you don't really know the difference. You've been listening to your unconscious mind, which has been giving you all these thoughts, wishes, dreams, and beliefs for so long that when inspiration seems to come through, you can't always tell the difference.

I've taught myself how to tell the difference, and I think I can tell you how. The biggest difference has to do with how you feel with different thoughts. With inspiration, there's usually a bit of a glow. Your feeling is up; your happiness is up; your excitement is up; your enthusiasm is up. That kind of energy usually doesn't come from your own deep-seated thoughts and wishes.

At first, when you're paying attention to your thoughts, wishes, and inspirations, you may not be sensitive enough to tell the difference. But as you stay with this, and you keep doing all of the clearing processes I've been teaching you, you'll get to the point where you can say, "That was inspiration," or "That was my unconscious mind daydreaming."

How do you tell the difference between inspiration and deep-seated thoughts and wishes? Again, go back through this book, continue to do the clearing processes, become more and more aware of and awake to your own thoughts, and you'll get closer to hearing inspiration. When you do, you'll feel it. It'll feel exciting, and you'll want to jump up and take action to implement the law of attraction and the law of creation.

How does taking inspired action affect the law of attraction?

As I've already pointed out, the word *action* is right in the word *attraction*. When you take inspired action, you accelerate the process of manifesting whatever you want. When you take action, you're engaging the law of creation and combining it with the law of attraction to bring what you prefer to have into your life. When you move into the abundance paradigm, all of this becomes automatic; it becomes your new way of being.

When you first started this book, you had one mind-set, which was unconscious: you didn't really think about beliefs. With the abundance paradigm, you move into an entirely different way of thinking about the world. From that place, the law of attraction and the law of creation work hand in hand; they're pretty easy and effortless, because you use them in same way you do your breathing.

How does taking inspired action affect the law of attraction? It speeds it up. That's the bottom line. If you want faster results, take action.

Of course, anybody could take action, so I should clarify what I mean by inspired action. Inspired action is when some idea seems to come from a higher or deeper part of you. There's something that nudges you, that says, "Do this," "Buy this," "Get this," or "Act on this." When you get that nudge from within, it's more than an action; it's an inspired action.

When you're in the abundance paradigm, virtually everything you do is going to come from inspired action. You're not really thinking about it anymore—you're certainly not worried about it—but you're taking inspired action, which, of course, speeds up the law of attraction.

Do I need to get totally clean and clear to receive inspiration, especially on a regular basis?

Absolutely not. You do not need to be totally clean and clear to receive inspiration. Inspiration is knocking on your door right now. It's trying to send you a message. The universe, the Divine, the whiteboard is always trying to send a signal to you, and it's a two-way street. You can send signals back to it in the form of requests or prayers, but you can also send them in the form of cleaning to clear the communication channel so the universe can hear your request and you can hear the inspiration coming from the Divine itself.

Do you need to be totally clean and clear? No. I'm not sure I know anybody who is totally clean and clear. Even Dr. Hew Len isn't finished. He's been doing this material for twenty-five years. He is far more advanced, he's in a far more abundant place, he's probably living from the abundance paradigm, but he will openly tell you he is still cleaning and clearing today.

Once I was on a radio show where somebody called in and said, "If I have to clean and clear forever, it's going to feel depressing that I never get to stop."

I thought about that and said, "The feeling of it being depressing is what you want to clean and clear on. You want to heal the thought that it's a burden for you to spend time going through these processes, because for me, the clearer you get, the happier you get, the more abundant you get, the wealthier you get, the healthier you get. Why not do it when the payoff is so incredible?"

Some might also complain that it's hard to use these cleaning and clearing techniques. But one is so easy that all you do is say, *I'm sorry. Please forgive me. Thank you. I love you.* In another, all you have to do was sit back and listen to a Sanskrit chant as it cleans and protects you. So how hard is it to continue the cleaning and clearing?

Do you have to be totally clean and clear to receive inspiration? No. You just have to be open to receiving it. You just have to spend time imagining the inspiration that is trying to come through. When it comes through, kick in the law of attraction and the law of creation, and take action to make it happen.

What am I to do or think if I follow inspiration, or what I thought was inspiration at the time, and things turn out badly as a result?

When I see a question like this one, I ask what stage of awakening it came from. Look at it again. Does that sound as if this person is awakened? Does it sound as if the person has surrendered? Does it sound as if the person is empowered, or does the person sound like a victim? When I hear this question, I hear a victim. This is a person who is afraid of the future, afraid to trust the Divine to give him or her some inspiration that's going to make a difference. This is a flag or a signal that this person is still thinking from a victim mentality.

Again, you want to go through all four stages of awakening and end up living the abundance paradigm, which is what this whole book is about.

What are you to do or think if you follow inspiration and it turns out badly? You shift it. Think it is going to turn into something good. In my program *The Secret to Attracting Money*, I said, "Take every experience and turn it into something good."

The only reason you call an experience bad is that you have judged it that way. If you saw the bigger picture, if you looked at it in a year or five years, you would be able to look at it and say, "I see the positive reason for it. Maybe there was a learning experience, a growth experience. Maybe it led to a left turn or right turn that actually turned into an abundance paradigm of its own. Who knows?"

This process involves trust. You have to follow inspiration, because inspiration knows what's better for you, more than your ego does. Inspiration is coming from the Divine, and your ego is giving you what it sees with its limited perception. Drop fear, drop the ego, come from inspiration, follow inspiration, and trust what happens.

How can I have more constant inspiration in my day-to-day life and decision making?

The easiest thing to do is meditate more: create an opening in your life to receive inspiration. Too many of us are like puppets, having our strings pulled by our cellphones, emails, faxes, computers, TV, radio, other people, and so on. We are being pulled around like robots whose buttons are being pushed. However, if you can separate yourself from that noise and stress, you make time to receive inspiration, which is always trying to come to you.

Almost every night when I'm home in Texas, I'll get in the hot tub. I'll relax underneath the Texas stars, look into the sky, and let go. I'll practice gratitude, going through all the things I'm grateful for, and I will wait. More often than not, inspiration comes for a book, a blog post, a new recording, something for my Miracles Coaching students—any number of things might come in. It could be a new idea for a business, a product, or a service. It could be for me to make a phone call. I can't predict it, and I don't want to. Predicting it means that I'm using the ego to guess what's in the future for me. But if I relax and allow inspiration to come, I could be surprised by something far juicier and more abundant than my ego ever could have imagined.

How can you have more constant inspiration in your day-to-day life and decision making? Take a deep breath, make time to relax, clean your mind to the best of your ability, get back to the whiteboard, and see what you're inspired to do.

Are there significant moments you can remember in your life when you recognized and followed inspiration? What was the result?

I was homeless for a long time when I was in Dallas decades ago. When I went to Houston, I was in poverty for about ten years. There was a great deal of struggle and strife. Inspiration and intuition were always knocking at my door, but I didn't answer, because I was afraid. I remember being told to do things like apply for a particular job, but I thought, "They'll never hire me. I'm homeless." Or my inspiration would tell me to go to a particular place of work that was looking for employees, but my mind said, "I'm in poverty; I can't even afford the car to go there," and I talked myself out of it. I would find ways not to follow inspiration. The longer I avoided the help that was coming from the Divine, the longer I stayed in the scarcity mindset. I never even dreamed of such a thing as an abundance paradigm. I was coming from the victim mentality.

When I started to slowly pay attention to intuition and inspiration, things started to become very different. At one point I was working for an oil company in Houston. Like everybody else, I always went to the mall to have lunch. But one day, inspiration said, "Turn left." I had no idea why, but I said, "OK. I'll follow this time," and I turned left. I went a couple of blocks, and there was an Italian deli. I grew up on Italian food in Ohio. I missed it. I didn't get it in Texas—not the kind I had back home.

This deli was run by a little Italian man, with whom I felt an immediate rapport. He made me a sandwich; it was incredible. I took it back to my office and told everybody about it. I was so impressed that I ended up making menus for him and giving them to him as a gift. I spread the news about the menu and the food around the oil company, and the deli owner and I became lifelong friends.

It didn't end there. Even though I was working for that oil company, I was still struggling and very unhappy. I needed a place to live. But my credit was bad; I didn't have the money; I didn't have the down payment. I was crying the blues to this Italian deli owner. He told me that his home, which was built for him, was for sale. He ended up owner-financing it for me when I desperately needed it. My wife at that time and I moved in; we lived there for years, and she lived there until her death. All because I followed inspiration and turned left one day, when everything else in me said, "Just do what you've always done before: go to the mall and have something to eat." Learn to follow inspiration and learn to trust it.

Are there any specific techniques to help keep calm in the face of anxiety around negative outside influences?

Obviously, there are many different techniques. Which are my favorites? The first one I like to use is the Emotional Freedom Technique (EFT)—the tapping technique. You can learn about it by watching the movie *The Tapping Solution* (formerly called *Try It on Everything*). I'm in that movie, teaching the technique. Or visit these websites: tryitoneverything.com and thetappingsolution.com.

First, realize that you're feeling anxious. In that moment, begin tapping your left hand on the underside. (This is the part that you would use for a karate chop.) Then say something to this effect: *even though I feel anxious right now, I deeply love, accept, and forgive myself.* That's all you have to say. Say it and repeat tapping: *Even though I feel anxious, I deeply love, accept, and forgive myself. Even though I feel anxious, I deeply love, accept, and forgive myself. Even though I feel anxious, I deeply love, accept, and forgive myself.* I say it three times.

If I'm about to give a speech or go on TV or if I'm doing a movie or some other event where I feel my anxiety go up, one of the first things I do is what I've just taught you: I tap the underside of my palm and say, *even though I feel anxious, I deeply love, accept, and forgive myself.*

The inventor of EFT was Roger Callahan, who originally called it Thought Field Therapy (TFT). It later evolved into EFT. It's one of my favorite things to do to reduce anxiety when everything seems to be swirling out of control. If you can be the center of the cyclone, you can do extremely well, and you can be the pillar of strength while everybody else is folding.

The second thing that I do is take a deep breath and touch something concrete in my environment, reminding myself that I'm in the moment. In the moment, everything's perfect. In the moment is the abundance paradigm. I take a deep breath, and I touch. Everything's OK, and now I'm centered. I'm back here.

I will also take long, deep breaths. I'll take in a breath, hold it for a second, and then slowly let it out. I might even count to six while I'm doing it, which forces me to slow down my breathing, because most people start to hyperventilate if they start to feel anxious. They bring in too much oxygen, which goes to their head. The next thing you know, they feel faint.

The final, bonus technique I'll give you for this question is to remember the what-if-up thinking that I've told you about in chapter 1. Change the thoughts that are bothering you—the nervous thoughts, the scary thoughts, the thoughts that are saying, "What if this all fails? What if I pass out when I'm going to speak? What if I feel anxious and have a heart attack?" Turn those into what-if-up thoughts: "What if this all works out? What if it's all fine? What if I'm totally healthy? What if there's no problem at all? What if this is going to be the best moment of the day? What if this is the way I'm going to shift into the abundance paradigm and experience prosperity in this moment? What if this is easy?"

When you do the what-if-up process, your energy and enthusiasm go up, and you feel different; you dispel the anxiety.

What is the best way to approach people about their negativity and faultfinding without offending them?

It's an interesting question, because there's a certain amount of ego involved when you say to somebody else, "Look, you are negative, and you have faults. I'm telling you about them as a gift."

If you've been reading this book up to this point, you know that everybody you see on the outside is a reflection of you. They are a mirror of the inside of you. Whatever you see as negativity or faults in them—sorry to say it, but those faults are in you.

This is all about 100 percent responsibility. It's not about other people. It's about you. You will experience the abundance paradigm all the faster as soon as you own everything in your particular reality.

Remember, you used the law of attraction to bring these other people into your life. Remember that because of the law of creation, you cocreated them in your experience; you took some action that helped bring them into your life orbit. They're there because of you. Maybe you did this on an unconscious level, but they're there as a gift.

Your ego is trying to judge these people, saying, "They've got negativity. They've got faults. How do I politely tell them?" You have to turn that around and say to yourself, "You have negativity. You have faults." That's the great quantum leap of learning.

How do you handle this? By going through the exercises I've given you earlier, by using all of the clearing and cleansing methods I've been teaching you throughout this book. Go back to your favorite ones, the ones that felt the easiest to you, the ones that had the most results for you, and do them over and over again. The healing and clearing to be done in the world has nothing to do with anybody else; it has everything to do with your perception of everybody else. If you're perceiving somebody else as negative and full of faults, that's what you have, and you need to clean it. That's not a problem, it's not something you blame yourself for, but you do have to take responsibility for it and handle it.

How do you stay happy and calm no matter what other people are doing, particularly when the other people are your spouse or other family members, and they are negative, crabby, and faultfinding?

This is very similar to the question I've just answered, but let me give you some more practical tips. Look in the mirror and say, "You've got to own that everything you see as faults, negativity, and crabbiness in other people is in yourself." Instead of trying to clean the other people, which is like trying to shave your mirror in the morning, you want to shave your own face.

How do you stay happy and calm? You create a support system. You surround yourself with success literature and read it all the time. You listen to success audios over and over again.

You also want to create a support group, meaning a Master Mind alliance. I wrote a book with Bill Hibbler called *Meet and Grow Rich*. It's all about how to create, form, and manage your own Master Mind group. A Master Mind is a group of five or six people (usually not less, usually not more, but it can vary) who are all there to support one another in achieving their dreams. It is a support group. If you create a support group, you now have a new family to support you.

The people who go into my Miracles Coaching Program get a miracles coach. That's part of their support system. You want to do the same thing in your own life. You're going to get better results when you have a support system or a coach.

Stay happy, stay calm, no matter what other people are doing, because that's the essence of living the abundance paradigm. But if you need help, create your own support system with reading material, listening material, and other people.

At what point do I sever relationships with friends and acquaintances to avoid negativity?

In many ways, you should never have to sever a relationship with friends to avoid their negativity. Instead you should be working on the negativity within you. In my life over the decades in which I've been learning spirituality and going through my own personal transformation, I've found that the people that were friends at one point in life just kind of left. I didn't have to sever relationships. We just moved on in different ways. There was no animosity, there was no fighting, there was no disagreement. We didn't call each other up and say, "Hey, I'm on a higher level of awareness than you, so goodbye." None of that took place. Instead we just went our own ways.

I think that's the wisest answer to this question. If you're in an abusive relationship with a friend, you may have to draw the line and do something about it. But I don't hear that in this particular question. I hear that somebody is trying to avoid negativity. Rather than avoid it, you want to clear it, because the negativity you see in others is, again, the negativity in you.

In order to use the law of attraction and the law of creation, you have to understand that you are attracting and creating everything in your life. It's all stemming from the mental mindset that you have right now. As you clean and clear it, you're going to shift it and live the abundance paradigm. You won't even see the negativity anymore, because it won't exist in your reality.

You may remember several questions I posed at the end of chapter 2. Now we're going to dive deeper in understanding them in order to fully explore the abundance paradigm.

Once I am cleared of major blocks, does inspiration naturally flow to my consciousness, or are other steps necessary?

No other steps are necessary. Once you are cleared of major blocks, inspiration is going to naturally start bubbling up. You'll get inspiration, you'll get intuition, you'll get feelings that you'll act on; there won't be anything to prevent you from acting on them, because the fears will be dissolved and dissolving.

If there's anything to do here, it's to continue clearing and cleaning any other beliefs or blocks that might still arise. Once you're cleared of the major ones, inspiration comes to you as a gift.

What is the difference between inspiration and regular thoughts?

Inspiration comes from the Divine and usually has some energy to it; it has a happy feeling. Regular thoughts pass through your brain like birds flying through the sky. There's no real energy to them. One thought might feel a little different than another, but in general, they're simply thoughts. They're just words, images, feelings going across the landscape of your brain. Inspiration usually has a bit of emotion to it—good emotion, a bit of spiritual energy.

As you go through all of these processes, you'll become more sensitive to the difference between inspiration and regular thoughts, and you'll learn to follow inspiration more and more.

How can I foster further inspiration once I have received it?

The easy answer is, use the law of creation: take action. The best way to further inspiration is to acknowledge the inspiration you're already getting. The law of attraction will allow inspiration into your life because you have stated that you want it. You've stated that you want it because you're going through this whole book, which is about the law of attraction. But the law of creation is waiting for you to take action. As soon as you receive inspiration, acknowledge it; that will reinforce the law of attraction to bring you more of it. But also take action on the inspiration. This will tell the universe you want more of it, and it'll start coming on a regular basis.

Why do blocks keep inspiration from happening?

Blocks represent fears. Inspiration is trying to come through, but it's as if you had put up a lead wall that says, "Not welcome here." The inspiration isn't going to come through. Why would you put up that lead wall? Because you're afraid. You're either afraid of failure or afraid of success: one or the other.

Almost everybody has a fear of failure, but you have to realize that there is no such thing as failure. You may get a result that you don't prefer, but I've learned that if you take that result and learn from it, you turn what looked like a failure into a success.

I've talked to a billionaire who declared bankruptcy a couple of times, and he said he realized something profound from failure.

"What was that?" I asked.

He said, "Nothing bad happens to you from failure."

When you realize that, you drop the block around failure.

But what about the fear of success? What about the block that says, "I don't want inspiration, because if I act on this and it works, I'll be a success, and what then?" Often people are afraid of success because it will change their life in a way they're not used to. It takes them out of their comfort zone, so they're afraid of it. Even though they want more, people don't usually want to leave where they are, because they're comfortable there. Where they are is the known; where they want to go is the unknown. It's often easier to stay where they are than to move forward and be a success.

I had to deal with this issue. I realized that the more successful I became, the more I could help myself, the community, and the country. I could make a difference in other people's lives. I could have a great life, and I could help other people have great lives. The more I looked at success and realized it was a good thing, the more I could have it in my life.

You want to drop all blocks to inspiration. Inspiration is the Holy Grail here; it is the fire of God; it is the Divine breathing through you; it is what you get when you live the abundance paradigm. You want to drop the blocks and the fears that are between inspiration and you. How do you do that? Through the cleaning and clearing sessions I've already taught.

When I follow inspiration, will I still get resistance?

Maybe, but only if there is still some resistance within you. If you start to follow inspiration and you hit a doubt or fear, all that means is that it's up for you to clean and clear. You attracted it, you created it, and it's time for you to erase it.

Some resistance may show up, but it is coming because you are moving into a different world. You're now becoming a different person. You're growing and transforming. The old you is leaving, and as you go into your transformation, some of this new you doesn't need the old you, but it might still have some resistance because it wants to stay with the old. Look at it as it comes up, and let it go. Release it, clear it. You want to be free. You want to be able to follow inspiration with no resistance. But if some shows up, it's OK. Just clean it, clear it. Use the processes we've already gone through.

Can we be inspired to do something that may not be best for us or that can even hurt us?

Again, look at the question. It's not coming from a higher stage of awakening; it's coming from the first stage, from victimhood. It's coming from somebody who's worried: will I be safe if I follow inspiration?

The first level of answering this question is to realize where the question came from. It's coming from a program, from a belief.

The second level of answering this question is no: you cannot be inspired to do something that is not good for you. The Divine is protecting you. God is protecting you. The whiteboard is protecting you.

You want to follow inspiration with deep trust, knowing that all is well and that all is even going to be better than what you have right now, if you continue to follow inspiration. In the abundance paradigm, you live from inspiration. You drop worry and concern about safety, because you know with a deep trust that you are protected.

Once I am inspired to do something, how can I keep myself from getting in the way or sabotaging my own success?

You have to remain focused on the inspiration. I don't say remain focused on the goal, because the goal may change, but the inspiration is always there. The Divine, the whiteboard, sent you this energy and said, "Go forth and do such and such." As you move in that direction, it will support you; it will give you little signs that say, "You're on the right track."

If along the way you feel you have hit a bump on the road, ask, "Am I sabotaging myself, or am I being told to turn left or turn right? Am I being told that I have to stop and regroup?"

You're being asked to follow inspiration no matter what, but the inspiration is the goal. You don't set a goal out there like saying you want so many sales within a ten-day period (although the inspiration might tell you to make so many phone calls). Follow the inspiration. That will keep you from getting in your own way.

Once the door of inspiration opens up, will it close if I don't act immediately?

Yes and no. It won't close entirely, because the inspiration is still there; you're still going to have it as a memory days, weeks, months from now. But if you don't act on inspiration almost instantly, the fire and energy that come from it won't last. You won't have the energy that came with the idea to help you carry it out.

The law of attraction will bring the inspiration to you, but you have to use the law of creation to bring it into being right now. If you don't, all is not lost, but you lose momentum. You could lose much of the energy that came as a gift from the inspiration.

When inspiration comes, take action. Use the law of attraction and the law of creation, which will take you to the abundance paradigm.

6

Limiting Beliefs about Money

Next we're going to talk about limiting beliefs about money. Again, these are questions that have come directly from the students in my Miracles Coaching Program. They're very real, very raw, and very sincere.

How can we say money is in infinite supply when the universe can't just print more in the basement? They only print so much.

First of all, the universe can and does print more money all the time. In fiscal 2020, the U.S. Bureau of Engraving and Printing printed 1.58 billion $1 notes and 1.33 billion $100 notes. (Of course, old or worn-out currency is being burned or recycled, so they do need to produce new bills.) So yes, the universe, in the form of the U.S. government, is printing more money.

When you hear questions like this, again, ask yourself what level they are coming from. Somebody who says, "The universe can't just print more money in the basement" is coming from the idea that there's scarcity; there isn't enough. They're in the first stage of awakening, the victim mentality.

When you hear a question like this, you have to remind yourself that in the abundance paradigm, there is no lack and limitation; there is no scarcity. Once you move into the abundance paradigm, you realize that money is really an invisible energy system that we agree on as a means of exchange; whenever you need more money, you just dip into the well of prosperity and pull it to you, using the law of attraction and the law of creation.

Again, look at where you're coming from with your questions. Are you coming from one of the first stages of awakening, or are you trying to come from the fourth, where you are living the awakened life through the abundance paradigm?

Is it resistance if I sue somebody who owes me money? Should I just let it go, expecting the universe to make it up to me?

I don't want to tell you whether or not you need to sue anyone, but let me give you a higher perspective from the abundance paradigm. If there is no lack and limitation in the world, it doesn't matter where the money comes from. It can come to you through the person that owes it you, or you can let that go, and it will come from somewhere or somebody else.

In my opinion, letting go and trusting the universe is the best way to attract money to you. When you forgive other people, you drop your resistance to receiving money. When you demand that money comes to you in one particular way, shape, or form, or through one particular job or one particular sale or one particular person, you are limiting the universe. The universe can bring money to you in a wide variety of ways, including unexpected ones. But if your ego thinks it can only come from one person or one job, you have closed off all other doors.

I can't give you legal advice. I can't say, sue or don't sue, but I can say from an abundance paradigm, forgiving, letting go, and allowing are probably the better choices, trusting that the money will come in another way. This is probably the wisest choice of all.

Is it ever appropriate to file bankruptcy? Can that be an immediate relief while I'm attracting more money? You teach building an atmosphere of integrity, and I'm not sure bankruptcy is integrity. Won't it create bad karma and attract bad things to me?

No, it's not going to attract bad karma or any bad things to you unless you judge bankruptcy as bad for you or for other people. For me, bankruptcy is an agreed upon way of resolving a conflict. I filed for bankruptcy once when I was going through my poverty years in Houston. I didn't actually have to complete the bankruptcy. When I filed, the creditors stopped calling me, I stopped worrying about it, and everything just more or less dissolved. I think there's a metaphysical reason for that: from the perspective of the abundance paradigm, once I filed, I took the stress off my concern about money. When the stress was gone, money was available and started to come back into my life.

Is it ever appropriate to file bankruptcy? Sure. I don't know whether it is for your personally, but it can be a tool that you use. Many famous and wealthy people have filed bankruptcy or been in debt. It's not a bad thing.

Bankruptcy was created so that you'll have a way out and your creditors, the people you owe money to, have a solution to the debt on their books. It can bring relief to them and to you.

But the really important question is, how are you thinking about this? What is your state of awakening when you're considering bankruptcy? If you are considering it bad, you can end up attracting bad to you. I don't mean that to scare you; I mean it to awaken you. You want to come from a perspective of trust and abundance, realizing that bankruptcy can be good. I'm not telling you what to do here. I do suggest you get some advice from people who know about bankruptcy and your financial situation. On your end, work internally to clear up issues around the law of attraction and the law of creation, using the clearing and cleansing methods I've given you.

If I feel good while I'm broke, won't that bring more of the same situation into my life? More of being broke?

No. I'm not asking you to feel good about being broke, but to feel good about certain things in your life that you genuinely appreciate. You can be grateful for the fact that you're alive, that you have a car, a roof over your head, or a refrigerator with something in it. There's something in your immediate environment that you can be happy about, even though on another level, you might feel you're broke. You're not giving thanks for being broke; you're giving thanks for something else in this moment for which you are genuinely grateful.

The more you can feel abundance right now, the more you will move into the abundance paradigm. It doesn't matter if you consider yourself to be broke. It doesn't matter if you have no money in your bank account and only a few dollars in your pocket, because if you can find the abundance of this moment, you will change the banking account and what's in your pocket. You'll do it through the law of attraction, through the law of creation, through all the exercises and processes you've been learning in this book. It's not a matter of feeling good about being broke, but appreciating where you are right now so you can attract more to appreciate. That's the big difference.

Will the universe always bring me money in the way I can imagine, or could it come in some other way that I haven't thought of yet?

Most of us, coming from the ego, think money has to come from a particular source, but that's not the truth. The universe can delight you and surprise you. You can end up creating a product or service or inventing something or winning something. There are so many possibilities for how money can come to you that I wouldn't suggest that you spend time imagining it; I would focus on feeling abundant right now. As you get ideas, take inspired action, using the law of creation and the law of attraction to bring them into being. The more you do, the more you'll have money coming into your life. You don't need to focus on money per se, and you don't need to focus on how it's coming to you in any specific way. Allow the universe to surprise you. There's nothing more delightful than unexpected income, and that's entirely possible as you move into the abundance paradigm.

I know I could make money if I had some seed money with which to get started. Can you suggest any sources where

I can borrow or partner with someone who has money to lend? Is that one of the ways the universe could bring me money?

It's certainly one of the ways the universe could bring you money. I don't know you personally, so I can't tell you whom to go to or partner with, but if you do a little research, you can find out on your own. You might begin by going to the bank or the Small Business Administration or Googling the subject online. There are countless stories of people who have done this: they started with nothing but managed to attract money into their lives.

I think it's more important that you be clear about what you want and be positive that you can have it. Use the law of attraction to make sure you are drawing everything and everybody into your life that's a match for what you want. Then, using the law of creation, act on the ideas that come to you to manifest what you need.

Here's a startling statement: sometimes you don't need any money to make these things happen. Sometimes focusing on the belief that you need money stops you from taking action right now. So I'll challenge you and say if you have an idea, ask, where can you start to create it, using the law of creation right now in this moment, whether you have money or not? Isn't there something you can do, somebody you can call or write to, or some organization you can contact? There's bound to be something you can do in this moment to begin to attract what you need. Money isn't always what you actually need.

If something moves my life mission forward but I can't really pay for it right now, is using a credit card OK, or do I have to wait until I have cash to pay for it?

Again I can't make a judgment call on your personal situation. I have heard about one way to handle credit cards: use only one card, put it in a glass of water, put it in the freezer, and freeze it. Whenever you are tempted to use the card, you're going to have to wait for it to thaw out before you can get to it. This will give you time to think about whether you want to make the purchase or not. It will slow down tapping out your credit card by acting too quickly.

Also remember that you don't always need money to implement your life mission, but you do need to take action. That's why I have focused so much on the law of creation. Far too many people haven't taken action to create anything. They've been sitting, they've been visualizing, they've been saying their affirmations as a mantra, but they've been clicking their heels together and hoping that magic will happen without their doing anything. The law of creation says that life is a cocreative process. You must help: you have to actually do something.

Maybe this means using a credit card, but don't make an instantaneous decision about that. Yes, there are many stories of people who started out by tapping out their credit cards; that's where they got their source funding. You're going to have to sit with that and be clear about what you want and the right move for you.

Another approach is to ask yourself whether using a credit card is the right thing to do. Reflect within yourself. What's the first feeling you get? Do you get, "Yes, that is the exact right thing to do; use the credit card"; "Maybe I should use the credit card, or maybe not"; or a flat-out "No, I should not use the credit card"? Unless you get an absolute yes, I'd say don't use that credit card, but again, this is for you to decide.

Now the very fact that the question is on your mind means that you have some doubts about using the card. If you have doubts, I'd say, don't use it. Remember, the law of attraction is going to bring a match to your vibration. If your vibration right now, your inner energy, is one of doubt, you're going to bring in more moments of doubt, so only use it if it's a big yes for you.

I'm seriously tempted to quit my job and start working a business idea that I have. It feels really risky but also really exciting at the same time. How can I be sure that it was really inspired? Also, is being inspired a guarantee of success?

Again, reflect on the question. Where is this person coming from? They're excited, so they're starting to feel empowered, which is the second stage of awakening, but they're also scared; they feel it's risky. They really want a guarantee of success. That's coming from the first stage of awakening, a victimhood mentality. This person is jumping between victimhood and empowerment, which is fine, but you want to go up the ladder of awakening to the abundance paradigm. You want to live in the fourth stage, which is the awakened mindset.

Should this person quit their job? I can't say whether they should or not. That's up to the person. But because they're asking, I would say probably not. I would start the business idea that they have while still working at their job.

This is common. When I worked for a big oil company back in Houston decades ago, I wrote my first books and my first articles on the company clock. While everybody else took breaks, I wrote my articles. While everybody else went to lunch, I usually stayed in the office and worked on my first book. Because I stayed at that job while pursuing my business idea, I was eventually able to get that first book published, way back in 1984, and I was able to feed myself and my family while it was going on, because I didn't quit my job.

Again, you have to check within yourself and find out: Is this a yes? Should I jump into doing this? Or is it a maybe, meaning you have hesitation, or is it a flat-out no, not at this time? You have to make that judgment for yourself, but do it with as much clarity as you can. Take a deep breath, sit with this idea, meditate on it, and maybe even ask for guidance. See what comes, then follow the guidance.

How long will it take after I stop feeling limiting beliefs until I see money coming in? Will it be a long time?

This question reflects a fear that money isn't going to come, or it is going to take a very long time; it might take forever. The reality is, money can come today. Money can come in the next few minutes. Money can come right now. Money can come tonight, tomorrow, next week. It will come when you are ready to receive it.

If a person has an unconscious belief that it takes a long time for money to arrive, guess what? The law of attraction is going to match that belief and make money take a long time. If you change that into a belief that money can come to me instantly, effortlessly, surprisingly, unexpectedly, and today, then guess what? The law of attraction will match that, and you can have money coming into your life by the time you finish reading this book. It's all a matter of a belief system.

I've said this for the longest time: change your beliefs, and you change your reality. When you move into the abundance paradigm, you move into a new reality that allows money to come to you while you sleep, while you work, while you eat, while you read. Money can come in any variety of ways, and it can come fast or slowly, depending on what you believe. If you believe that it takes a long time for money to come, realize that's a belief; it's not a fact. It is not true for everybody. It's something that you've created using the law of creation and something you've attracted using the law of attraction.

What do you about it? Go back and review your favorite clearing sessions from this book. That will help you break free.

How can I grow and find success in my life and being if I don't have belief in myself already?

I love that question, because I can relate it back to when I was homeless and in poverty. It felt as if it was me against the world. I felt I had no belief in myself, no self-esteem, and I wasn't going to make it, even though I was going to continue to scramble and try.

I learned that if you take little baby steps, if you start to move in a direction of the success you want and do something that's measurable, that's accountable, that you can tell other people about, you will begin to believe in yourself.

The first way to start this is to say, *I am going to achieve success* as an affirmation. Yes, it's new mind talk and yes, you're still on a lower level of awakening, but this is how you move up the ladder of consciousness. You start with your thoughts, and you start to change them.

As for the previous thoughts—I don't have the self-esteem, I don't have the success, I don't have a belief in myself—let's stop that circle of destruction right there and turn it into what-if-up thinking. Start to say, "I do have belief in myself, I am going to succeed, and I am going to take action on the first thing that comes to mind right now."

As you begin to take action, which is the core of the law of creation, you will start to get new results, and you'll start to feel better about yourself. Whenever you do the things you know you need to do, you will build self-esteem, you will build a new self-image, and you will empower yourself.

How do you start? You start right where you are. You don't have to wait for anything to change, because nothing is going to change until you do. It's all an inside job.

Look within your life and ask yourself what goal you want to achieve. If it's a huge goal, break it down. What's the tiniest first step you can take? If you want to write a book, maybe it's just turning on your computer and writing the title and the first line. After the first line, you write the second line. Slowly you build this new belief that you are an author and you are going to be published.

Maybe you want to be a speaker, an entrepreneur, or a small-business owner. Whatever it happens to be, write down the goal, and then break it into small steps. Pick the tiniest, safest, least risky step there is, the one you can do today, and start to do it. Over time you will build a new you.

I've heard it said that you can't truly love others until you love yourself. Is that an accurate statement?

The key word in this question is *truly*. You can't truly love others until you love yourself. When you love yourself, you have the capacity to understand, accept, love, and nourish other people. It does all begin with you. If you grasp the deeper lessons of this book, you will understand that the outer world is simply a reflection of your inner world. You don't want to begin by finding things on the outside to love; you want to begin by finding the inner you to love.

You will have the abundance paradigm as a permanent shift in consciousness if you understand one primary message: at the core of you, beyond your thoughts, your feelings, your worries, and all the other things going on in your awareness, is a witness. I've called it zero, God, the whiteboard, the Divine. That divine blank slate, that whiteboard of consciousness, the witness that's watching everything in your world, at the core is love. The more you can go to this inner essence of love within you, the more you'll be able to love yourself and others. It all starts within.

Is it possible to really love yourself when there are features of your own personality or body that you don't like, or is total and unconditional acceptance of self required?

You can love yourself just as you are *and* you can want to change. You can love yourself as a work in progress.

You can look at yourself and say, "I do like my shoulders, but I don't really care for my stomach, and I do like my legs, but I don't care for my feet." However, you are plastic in many ways: you can transform yourself physically into whatever you want. There are some physical limitations, of course, but we're talking about refining your body. Even that begins from the inside.

Here's the biggest clue to changing yourself: accept yourself. Begin by loving yourself. The more you can love yourself just as you are, the more you will morph into a perfect being. Perfection, of course is relative, but I mean it in the sense of a subjective awakening and self-description.

The more you can love yourself as you are, the more you will move into acceptance of yourself as you are. Then you will start to change those parts of you that you haven't liked in the past. But you do have to accept yourself as you are now. You are a work in progress, I am a work in progress, but I have found that I can speed up this work in progress if I love the work as it currently is.

You are the Michelangelo of your life, and you are the David that you are sculpting. When Michelangelo had that big piece of marble to begin with, he had to love it as it was in front of him; then he had to chisel away everything that wasn't David. The end result was a masterpiece that has stood for centuries.

You sculpt your own body into the life, being, and physical reality that you want, but it begins with acceptance and love. The core of the abundance paradigm is acceptance and love. If you want to come from the abundance paradigm when you're looking at your body, accept it and love it as you work on it.

I've been put down by my parents and others my whole life. How can I shed the negative self-image that I developed over the years so I can come to love and accept myself?

I can relate to that. I wrote a book about my upbringing called *Adventures Within*. I had a very abusive childhood and a father who was a bit of a terror. An ex-Marine and an ex-prizefighter, he ran his family as if it were a boot camp from the Korean War. It was tough going, but he was doing the best he could. He didn't have a manual on how to raise his children. He raised them based on the programming he had at that time. Most of it was military training or physical training from his boxing world.

Your parents were doing the best they could. From the viewpoint of the abundance paradigm, you have to understand that they weren't doing anything consciously to hurt or abuse you. You have to forgive them. The more you forgive them, the better you'll feel right now.

You have to go further and forgive yourself for having judged them for not raising you differently. You have to forgive them, and you have to forgive yourself. That's the first level of awakening.

On the second level, you want to realize that you've been telling yourself a story. We are storied beings: we make sense of our lives by telling stories that group all the facts in our journey to this moment.

However, you can tell a different story. I now tell the story that my parents were the best in the world. My father taught me strength. He taught me discipline. He taught me to be able to go for what I want and not to bow down to anybody. He taught me how to speak, how to be strong, how to stand up in the world. I got that from a father who in my previous story was the enemy, was abusive and difficult to live with, a disciplinarian who used physical strength to get people to obey.

It's the same father, but I've told a different story. Now the story is one of strength, and I have pride in telling it. My father is alive and well in his eighties. He's the Jack LaLanne of the family, exercising twice a day. I see him as an inspiration. Yet he's the same father I had when I was growing up.

You have a choice. It begins with forgiveness of your family and yourself and going on to create a new story. Just tell the story differently, in a positive light, and you'll shed the negative self-image and create a positive self-image, because the story will strengthen you.

I know others that also struggle with their self-worth. Is there anything I can do to help heal their image of themselves?

My bottom-line advice about persuading people is to be a source, a model, of inspiration to them. You don't necessarily try to heal anybody else. You always work on yourself; you always heal yourself. As you grow and transform, others will see you, and they will imitate your behavior.

Science is researching mirror neurons, meaning that we watch other people around us—not only family and friends, but the people close to us, those we see most often—and we mirror what they're doing. If you become a model of inspiration to other people, whether they have a strong self-image or not, they will start to imitate you unconsciously. You will influence them in a positive way.

I don't think you have to go to anybody and directly say, "Here's how to change." But you can change yourself, and as you do, others will see and mirror it. Also remember that from the abundance paradigm perspective, there is nobody to change. With anything you see on the outside that you don't like or that you feel needs to be polished, you do the changing and polishing and liking on the inside of you. Change, again, is an inside job.

Are there things that most people do on a regular basis that destroy their self-esteem without their realizing it? What are some of the actions or thoughts that I should be aware of?

Almost everybody knows when they're doing something that's not in their best interest. Whether they're trying to lose weight but reaching for the cake or they're trying to stop smoking but reaching for a cigarette, they know that that is not the life-affirming action they need to be taking. They have to go within themselves and be aware of whether their thoughts are propelling them to act on something they don't really want.

Now you know from all the work we've done together in this book that when you change your inside beliefs, you have a different reality. You want to look at the thoughts that are stimulating you to do something negative or harmful, and you want to change those thoughts, because they are the essence of the law of attraction. As you change your thoughts, you'll take a different action, which means the law of creation will kick in, and you'll bring yourself a different result.

Again, you'll have some work to do, but all it really means is having a razor-sharp awareness, a sensitivity to how you're thinking and feeling, and then pausing and asking yourself, "Is this a life-affirming thought? Is this an abundance maneuver? Or is it something I'm going to regret?" If you fear you're going to regret the next thought or the next move that you're going to take, find a way to stop it.

I don't want to oversimplify by just telling you to stop it, because I want to remind you that in this book, you have learned very powerful clearing processes. Use them. Go back to the ones that feel the best to you and do them on your own. Do something to get clear so that you can have strong self-esteem, which wants to follow the messages from the Divine.

How can I help to protect my child's self-image when the kids at school pick on them and are unkind?

You have to have a strong self-image of your own. If you're coming from a place of fear and overconcern, your child's going to pick up on that, and their own self-esteem is going to replicate yours. They will have a weakness about them that will show to other people. The other kids will pick on them, because the kids will read the energy signal from the child. The child is getting that energy signal from you, so the very question suggests that you have fear.

You want to clear the fear in yourself so you have more confidence about your child. Because of the mirror neuron effect, your increased confidence will spill down to your child, who in turn will have stronger self-confidence. As the child goes to school feeling this inner sense of security, the kids around them will not pick on them.

Again, you have to work on *you*. You don't have to work on your child. As you work on you, the child will note the difference and mirror it.

Dr. Hew Len was not a murderer. How did he attract murderers into his life? I'm having a hard time seeing the connection.

Dr. Hew Len was a therapist; he was studying murderers. He was studying people who committed violent crimes. Because he put so much time, effort, and enthusiasm into his research, he was bound to bring the people that matched it into his life. If he had been studying cooking, he probably would have pulled chefs into his life, but he wasn't. He was studying abnormal behavior; he was studying violent criminals. Because of that focus, he attracted murderers, who were in the mental hospital that he worked in.

Understand the deeper levels of this idea. The law of attraction says you are going to get what you focus on with energy and enthusiasm. Whenever you put a lot of emotion on—which usually means whatever you really love or whatever you really fear or hate—is going to show up in your life. That's the law of attraction.

I'm encouraging you to love more; come from love. Love is the heart of the abundance paradigm. In this paradigm, love is what you see when you look around. If you love where you're at right now, the law of attraction says you'll get more of it. If you love the very thing that you would like to have in your life, a person, place or thing, the law of attraction says you will begin to attract it into your life.

Of course you also have to use the law of action and do something to make this happen. Dr. Hew Len was studying these kinds of people, and the law of attraction said, "OK, you want to know more about these people. We will present you with a situation where you can learn more."

Then he learned that there was an opening at the state hospital in Hawaii. He used the law of creation, meaning he had to fill out an application, turn it in, make a phone call, fly to Hawaii, and have an interview.

These elements all reveal how to make your life work. What are you focused on? The law of attraction is going to match it. What are you taking action to do or not to do? The law of creation is going to help you manifest it.

Sometimes I have panic attacks about money. I am doing ho'oponopono, I am doing my what-if-upping, but money still haunts me. Is it just that it will take time to manifest? How can I feel good while I wait?

This question suggests that the person is still concerned. What does that mean? There's still a belief in their mind—whether it's unconscious or conscious—that money is not going to come. The person needs to clear and clean those limiting beliefs.

What do you do while you're waiting for the situation to change? You don't wait: you use the law of creation; you take action. Go back to one of your favorite clearing practices from this book and redo it. Redo it every day if you have to so you can get rid of the haunting feeling and the negative belief.

If you're wondering how you can feel good while you wait, you practice gratitude. Again, you have to look around in your environment, find something that you are genuinely grateful for, and focus on it. The more you can focus on gratitude, the more abundant you will feel. The more abundant you feel, the more the law of attraction will bring you the wealth you need to match that feeling.

So you do have some work to do, but you can probably take care of this issue by repeating the clearing practice of your choice once or twice more.

I want it now; I need it now. Why isn't the money coming? I've been studying the law of attraction for years; it doesn't feel like it's working. Is this normal?

It's only normal to the extent that you have a desperate feeling about money. I've had this feeling. I've been at points in my life where I thought, "I'm doing everything right. I'm reading the metaphysical books and the success literature, and I'm taking action. Where is the money?"

What I didn't understand at the time—and what most people don't understand—is that the law of attraction was matching my unconscious belief system. This is what I described in my audio program *The Missing Secret*, which says the law of attraction matches your unconscious beliefs, not your conscious beliefs. When somebody is saying, "I need money," what is the energy behind that? It's desperation. So what's the law of attraction is going to match? Desperation.

In order for this to change, you have to relax into the moment, and again, abundance is in this moment. When you look at this moment and you say, "Where's the money?", you're not seeing the abundance. You're seeing the scarcity. You're coming from an old mindset and an old paradigm. You want to shift into the new paradigm. Once you do, you'll turn around and say, "There's abundance everywhere." Because you see abundance everywhere, the law of attraction and the law of creation will bring money and money opportunities into your next moment.

Even though I identify with this questioner, they need to disconnect the fear that money isn't going to come, because that fear is going to push it away.

I feel attached to the outcome. My business has to work. How can I be unattached to the outcome and still believe at the same time?

You have to do a balancing act within yourself, saying, "I believe in my vision, and if for some crazy reason it doesn't work out the way I envision it, it will work out in some other, even better way."

This is a new mindset for most people, because they think, "The business has to work out or I will fail; I will be destroyed; I will be on the streets." Obviously that thought is not oriented toward the abundance paradigm. Again, this is all about shifting perception, shifting beliefs. Instead of coming from fear and scarcity, you want to come from power, and you want to come from trust.

How do you detach from the outcome? Someday I'm going to write a book called *Mystic in the Marketplace*. It would be based on the idea that as you go about your business and trying to manifest what you want, you remain detached from it. As I've already said, one way to find the abundance paradigm and to go to Source is to observe that you're not your thoughts, you're not your feelings, you're not your body, and you're not your actions. You are a witness behind and within all of that.

You can become a mystic in the marketplace if you can take that mindset into the business world. This is entirely possible. You might need to put a little card on your desk that says, "Remember, mystic in the marketplace." Whenever you see it, take a deep breath and say, "OK, what I'm doing is not me. I'm doing it, using the law of creation, but I am detached from it, because I'm coming from the abundance mindset."

So you take action; yes, you want everything to work out. You are optimistic; you're doing the right stuff. The law of attraction is on your side, and you are detached, knowing that the universe, the Divine, God is taking care of you. That's the balancing act that you need to perform.

When you have it, you will accomplish more faster and will be more successful.

If I have a few negative thoughts throughout the day but shake them out of my head and start thinking positive again, have I screwed up my life because I've had those negative thoughts?

No, not at all. The universe has put a wonderful fail-safe system into our body and mind. It says that what you think about right now, with energy and focus, will tend to come about in the next three days or so.

We have thoughts all day long. I saw one statistic that said we have sixty thousand to eighty thousand thoughts a day. It's a good thing they all don't manifest immediately, because they're not all very wholesome. Many of them are negative and trashy.

You want to do what you're doing: shake them out of your head and focus on the positive. Do what-if-up thinking, and change those thoughts into ones you prefer. Focus on what you will to accomplish, remembering that the law of attraction is going to match what you're thinking and feeling on an unconscious level.

Don't worry about negative thoughts. If they come, just say, "Hey thanks," then let them go. When positive thoughts come, put some juice into them. Focus on them, because the thoughts that you focus on are the ones that are going to come about in the next few days to a week.

My family doesn't support me, but I have to be around them all the time. How can I feel good anyway?

The easy answer is, of course, read books like this one. Listen to self-affirming audios. Surround yourself with positive people. You can in a way create a whole new family.

I grew up in Ohio. I left at one point and went to Texas. It was a turning point in my life, because I cut ties in many ways. Not that I turned my back on my family: I still have my family, and I still had them back then. But because I left them, I had to create a new family in Texas.

There was a lot of struggle during that time, but only because I didn't know about inspirational books like this one or inspirational audios. They weren't available all those decades ago—at least not in my awareness. But I created a new support system, friends who believed in me, a new Master Mind group. Although I didn't know what a Master Mind was at that point, I learned how to create one and created a whole new family because of it.

Now that I've said all of that, you also want to be immune to what your family is doing or not doing. Again, detachment is one signal that you're in the abundance paradigm. Detachment means that they can say, do, or be whatever they want, but you're going to say, do, or be whatever you need to be, following your own inspiration. Whatever the family is doing or not doing—well, that's fine for the family. Focus on what's going on in you.

To take this to a higher level, if the family is pushing buttons within you, remember that those buttons aren't in your family, they're in you. So if they're saying something that's irritating you, use clearing practices to help you get through it. Heal on the inside, and you'll see your reality, including your family, change.

My husband thinks the law of attraction is phony-baloney. Sometimes it makes me mad that I can't share all the amazing stuff I'm learning with him. How can I get him to come onboard? What if I can't get him to change?

Think about the mentality that's behind this. First of all, if your husband thinks the law of attraction is phony-baloney, he's probably mirroring an aspect of you that also thinks it's phony-baloney. You might say that it's amazing stuff, but if the mirror that's in the form of your husband is saying this is all phony-baloney, most likely at least some sliver of a belief within you agrees with it.

Don't change him; change you. Go in and ask yourself, "Do I completely believe in the law of attraction?" If you get a yes, fine; you're done. But if you get a no that says, "I do have my doubts; I do at times think it's phony-baloney," then you want to ask yourself, "Why do I think that way? What's my evidence for it?"

You're unearthing your own support system for that negative belief. Look at that system, and question the evidence for it. When you do, it will disappear, and you'll know that the law of attraction actually works. When you know it with 100 percent integrity in yourself, most likely your husband will quit saying anything negative about it.

Also consider this: if you're walking around the house and getting mad because your husband isn't onboard with your belief system, what is he probably thinking about the law of attraction? He must think it doesn't work at all if you're getting so upset so easily.

Obviously, there's a button within you that is trying to persuade him to get onboard with you. Some button in you is saying, "I need him to believe like me; otherwise our whole relationship will fall apart." That's not true. You don't need him to be onboard. He is free to believe whatever he wants. But if he sees that you're walking around angry, he's likely to think, "This law of attraction doesn't work very well. Look how upset she is, and how easily."

I would invite you to do more clearing exercises. Go back to your favorite ones and do them again. Allow your husband to be whatever he wants to be, but make sure you are at peace within you. In the abundance paradigm, you're not going to be angry, mad, or jealous. You're not trying to change somebody so you feel better. In the abundance paradigm, you'll be coming from love and acceptance, but again, that begins in you.

I feel compelled by God to become a counselor. It excites me. But I'm sixty years old. Isn't it too late to go back to school? Do I have to have a degree? Can I find some way to do it without a degree? Would it be incredible? Making these decisions confuses me sometimes. Shouldn't the Divine give me a sign?

I think the Divine has already given you a sign. You began by saying, "I feel compelled by God to become a counselor." That sounds like a sign to me. So you are getting the inspiration to become a counselor. It feels to you that it came from God, and it probably did.

The law of creation says you now have to take action. You're obviously excited, yet you have the *but*: "But I'm sixty; isn't it too late?" These doubts are coming up from the part of you that isn't in alignment with this goal. You want to do clearing exercises on this feeling, because age doesn't matter. We know people that have gone into their eighties and nineties and started a new career, manifested something, or made a difference that has lasted forever.

Is it too late to go back to school? No. You can go back to school whenever you want. You can go online, or you can go to the brick-and-mortar schools; that's all available. It's all a choice.

Do you have to have a degree? I don't know what kind of counselor you want to be, so I can't answer that one. Could you do it without a degree? Again, it depends on what kind of counselor you want to be.

I think the bigger issue here is that you want the Divine to give you a sign, and it did. It said, "You put out a request," which engaged the law of attraction. The Divine said, "Here's your inspiration: become a counselor." But instead of engaging the law of creation and taking action, you let doubts come in.

Almost everybody does this, so you need to ask, "When was the last time I got an inspired idea, gave thanks for it, and got excited about it, but then talked myself out of it?"

This person is about to talk themselves out of becoming a counselor. Hopefully they have not. Hopefully they went back and did the clearing exercises. But if you are also in that boat, you also want to go back and do the clearing exercises, so you are free to use the law of creation to engage the inspiration that came to you and live out this new vision.

In the abundance paradigm, when you get an idea, you will act on it without doubt, without concern, without reservation. The doubts won't be there, because they no longer exist within you. The level of trust is so complete that there isn't anything left in there to say, "This won't work" or "No, not for me." So do a little bit of clearing work. Then follow your inspiration, use the law of creation, and take action.

I really can't see how I've created all this garbage in my life. People do lousy things, and I'm stuck holding the bag. I am a victim. How can I see it any other way?

What stage of awakening is this person coming from? They say it themselves: they're coming from the first stage. They are feeling like a victim. They are coming from a victim mentality. They know it, and they're owning it.

The belief that you're a victim is coming from a program that's not you. This is a breakthrough statement. It is the kind of insight that can pop you into the abundance paradigm right now. This person is not speaking as this person. This person is speaking a program or a type of virus of the mind that he or she happens to have.

Let me see if I can explain this another way. I was on a radio show one time where Dr. Hew Len and I were the guests. We were taking turns answering call-in questions, which were pretty blunt. Some were surprisingly negative, almost insulting. I apologized to Dr. Hew Len and said, "I'm sorry. I don't know who these people are or why they're calling like this."

Dr. Hew Len didn't miss a beat. He smiled and said, "Joe, it's not them. It's the program in them."

When I heard it, I thought, "What a tremendous insight!" People are often operating as machinery. We've been programmed to act and think and be in a certain way. Most of it is coming from lack, limitation, and scarcity. It is not coming from abundance or love. We have not been taught that way.

So when this person says, "I am a victim; how can I see any other way?" they're speaking the program that they have acquired in their life.

Now you, the reader, right now need to understand that this program is probably in you. Maybe you're not verbalizing it, but maybe you thought it at one point. You want to clear it. I am clearing it, because I stated this question, so it must be in me as well. Remember, we're creating our own reality using the law of creation and the law of attraction. What do we do? We erase it. *I love you, I'm sorry, please forgive me, thank you. I love you, I'm sorry, please forgive me, thank you.*

When we erase this question as it arises within us, we help erase it from the program in the person who asked it. We're saying to the Divine, "I'm sorry. I don't know where this program came from, but please forgive me, because I've been unconscious and it showed up in my life. It came from somewhere. Who knows and who cares? Thank you for removing it. Thank you for clearing it. Thank you for healing it." Then you say, "I love you" to the Divine, merging into the love, compassion, forgiveness, and acceptance that make everything wholesome again, that make everything the abundance paradigm. *I love you, I'm sorry, please forgive me, thank you.* What a wonderful way to end these questions.

*   *   *

Finally, to help you make the transformation that I've been describing, here are five ways to shift into the abundance paradigm.

The first one is a question: *how are you being?* Not doing, but being. Are you feeling fearful? Are you feeling empowered? Are you feeling surrendered? Do you feel you're letting go into the now? The more you can drop all the walls of fear, lack, and limitation, the more you can be abundant right now. Abundance is in this moment. As you settle into this moment, become very aware, very sensitive to the inside of yourself. How are you being? Do you feel that all is well? Do you feel you're still concerned about things?

Whatever you feel is OK, but the more you can move into a feeling of security, divine protection, opulence, and abundance, the more you can shift into the abundance paradigm.

If you don't feel that way right now, if you don't feel you're being abundant, what do you do? You can fake it until you make it. You can look around and start to find something to feel abundant about and grateful for. Maybe it's just remembering that in this moment all is well and abundance and gratitude exist. When you look out into the world and see it as half empty, you know which paradigm you're coming from. If you see it as half full and filling up, you also know which paradigm you're coming from.

Choose to come from the paradigm that says, "All is well. I am abundant, I live in abundance, and abundance is my birthright and my right in this moment. Right now, all is abundance." Move into that state of being where you're living the abundance paradigm.

The second way of shifting into the abundance paradigm is to ask yourself, *what are you seeing?* When you look around, what do you note? Do you see things that cause you to be concerned or fearful? Or do you see things that remind you that all is well, that there is abundance, that you are taken care of, that in this moment you have plenty to be grateful for, and more coming, because of the law of attraction and the law of creation?

You've probably seen that optical illusion drawing which, if you look at it from one mindset, resembles an old woman, but if you look at it from a slightly shifted mindset, the same image now resembles a young woman. That's how life is. You can look at it from a paradigm of lack and limitation or from a paradigm of abundance. What are you seeing?

Changing your paradigm is really a matter of a relaxed focus. That optical illusion picture is a single piece of art. But if you relax your focus, suddenly you see the other picture. It's been there all along.

That's how the abundance paradigm is. It's here. It's been here all along. You didn't see it because the glasses you were wearing were from a system of beliefs that were wired to see only scarcity. Now you are rewiring your mind to see abundance.

So what are you seeing? If you don't see the abundance right now, again, just fake it. Start to play with the possibilities. Look around at this world and say, "This is amazing! How was it created? How did this book get written? How did these ideas get to me?" There are true magic and miracles in the world, there is true abundance in the world, and you can start to see it when you choose to see it.

The third way to shift into an abundance paradigm is to ask yourself, *how are you acting?* Are you using the law of creation from fear or from trust? You know that the law of attraction is going to give you more of whatever you focus on. You know the law of creation is going to give you things to do. Are you going to do them? Do you talk yourself out of them? Do you receive inspiration but follow it with doubt, or do you follow it with action?

You might also ask yourself if you're coming from ego or Spirit. How are you acting in the world? Most people, of course, come from the ego. They want things, they demand things, they're afraid of things, they blame other people for their lives—that's all ego.

As you know, there are four stages of awakening, and most people are stuck in the first one: victimhood. Then there is the empowerment stage, but we don't stop there. There's still the stage where you surrender to the Divine.

At this point, however, we're focusing on the fourth stage: the stage of awakening, where you live the abundance paradigm.

How do you get there? One way is by how you act. First of all, most people don't even take action. You know by now the law of creation says you must cocreate everything in your life, meaning that you must take action. Yes, some things will magically appear in your life, but for the most part, you will be asked with a nudge from inspiration to do something to create your reality.

Are you acting? When you act, are you coming from fear or faith? Most people come from fear. They are afraid to take any action, or if they do, they do it with a certain nervousness. And of course the law of attraction says, "If you're coming from nervousness, we're going to match it and give you things to be nervous about." You want to come from faith. In short, you want to come from Spirit.

If that's not your experience right now, what do you do? Every time you have a moment of choice, take a deep breath and ask, what would ego do, and what would God, or Spirit, do? Choose the divine path. You may feel a little nervous at first because you are stretching out of your comfort zone, but that doesn't mean don't do it. It simply means it's new for you. As you make new movements and stretch out of your comfort zone, you will feel comfortable again.

So how are you acting? Are you coming from trust and faith? Are you coming from Spirit? Choose Spirit.

The fourth way to shift into an abundance paradigm is to ask yourself, *how or what are you thinking?* Do you have more fearful thoughts or positive thoughts? Do you have more fear-based concerns or what-if-upping thoughts?

In the ideal world, where you live the abundance paradigm, you don't even have thoughts. You may have flickers of awareness that fly across the whiteboard of your life, but you don't necessarily pay attention to them. You've learned to ignore thoughts and come from a place of no thoughts or no thinking.

Obviously, this doesn't mean turning off your conscious mind or bumbling your way through life. You are more aware and alert than you ever were before. In the abundance paradigm, you come from pure awareness. Thoughts may still come and go, but they're few and far between. You don't even necessarily pay attention to them, because you're living the breath of God through you.

What if this isn't true for you right now? How do you handle your thinking? The first thing to do is pay attention to it. Note what kind of thoughts you're having. Are they fearful thoughts or faithful thoughts? Are they down thoughts, which make you feel concerned about your next steps and your next moments? Or are they up thoughts, which help you feel better about this moment and about what's coming your way? You get to choose.

You can't predict what your next thought is going to be, but when it comes up, you can choose what to do with it. So how are you thinking? What are you thinking? When the thoughts come by, turn them into something magnificent. Turn them into something good: up those thoughts. As you're doing this, be aware that you are not your thoughts. You are what's behind the thoughts, witnessing them. The abundance paradigm exists in that background awareness—the whiteboard. When it's wiped clean of all thoughts, you live from inspiration, and the law of attraction and the law of creation are natural for you.

The fifth way for you to come from an abundance paradigm is to ask yourself a question I've already asked you in different forms throughout this book: *What is behind your thoughts, your feelings, your body, and your mind? What is behind it all?*

I saw a movie about Pope John Paul II that was called *Karol: A Man Who Became Pope*. In it he's having an argument with a Russian atheist, who is saying that there is no God and there's nothing out there; it's just all blank and void. The pope says, "What you call nothing is what I call everything."

I love that. "What you call nothing is what I call everything"—the whiteboard, the witness, the zero that's behind your thoughts, your feelings, your body, your mind, that's behind it all. That observer at the core of your being is the Divine, is everything. It is alive. It is alive in you, breathing through you.

The more you can move into that Spirit, the more you become the abundance paradigm. You no longer need clearing exercises. You no longer need tools. You no longer need tips or methods to help you stay the course, because you *are* the course. At that point, you are one with zero. At zero, there are no limits. At that point, you are one with the whiteboard. There is nothing written on the whiteboard, and you can have, do, or be whatever you can imagine, because what you're imagining is coming from the Source itself. At that point, you'll be on a mission from God.

What if this is not the case for you right now? What if you're still struggling with these ideas and you're not even really sure what's behind your thoughts, feelings, body, and mind? Simply use this as an exercise. Go back and do some of the clearing exercises I've given you, and use them to help you return to zero. Use them to get to the place where you can at last notice that behind your life is an emptiness that is really everything.

As you're reading these words, pause and ask yourself, what is doing the reading? As you're thinking, what's observing the thoughts? As you're feeling, what's noticing your feelings? As you're in your body, what's noticing your body? As you're paying attention to anything in your experience—your body, your mind, your thoughts, your feelings, your emotions—what is the thing in you noticing it all? What is the observer?

This Zenlike question will pull you into that background awareness. This background witness in you is also the same witness in me. It's the same witness in your neighbor, your coworker, your business partner, the people on the street. They don't know it, because they haven't had a clue that deep down within them is the abundance paradigm, and you get there by becoming aware of the Source of it all and that Source is God.

I want to thank you for reading this book. I encourage you to go back, reread your favorite parts, and redo the clearing and cleansing exercises. The more you do, the better you'll feel, and the more you'll be able to experience the reality of the abundance paradigm. Meanwhile, I encourage you to go for your dreams, follow your inspiration, and use the law of attraction and the law of creation to help you with everything you want in your life. Godspeed to you. I love you.

About the Author

r. Joe Vitale is a globally famous author, marketing guru, movie, TV, and radio personality, musician, and one of the top 50 inspirational speakers in the world.

His many bestselling books include *The Attractor Factor*, *Attract Money Now*, *Zero Limits*, *The Miracle: Six Steps to Enlightenment*, and *Anything Is Possible*.

He's also recorded numerous bestselling audio programs, from The Missing Secret and The Zero Point to The Power of Outrageousness Marketing and The Awakening Course.

A popular, leading expert on the law of attraction in many hit movies, including The Secret, Dr. Vitale discovered the "missing secret" not revealed in the movie. He's been on Larry King Live, Donny Deutsch's "The Big Idea," CNN, CNBC, CBS, ABC, Fox News: Fox & Friends and Extra TV. He's also been featured in *The New York Times* and *Newsweek*.

One of his most recent accomplishments includes being the world's first self-help singer-songwriter as seen in 2012's *Rolling Stone Magazine*. To date, he has released seventeen albums! Several of his songs were recognized and nominated for the Posi Award, regarded as "The Grammys of Positive Music."

Well-known not only as a thinker, but as a healer, clearing people's subconscious minds of limiting beliefs, Dr. Joe Vitale is also an authentic practitioner of modern Ho'oponopono, certified Reiki healer, certified Chi Kung practitioner, certified Clinical Hypnotherapist, certified NLP practitioner, Ordained Minister, and Doctor of Metaphysical Science.

He is a seeker and a learner; once homeless, he has spent the last four decades learning how to master the powers that channel the pure creative energy of life without resistance, and created the Miracles Coaching® and Zero Limits Mastery® programs to help people achieve their life's purpose. He lives in the Austin, Texas area, with bestselling author Lisa Winston.

His main site is www.MrFire.com.